CAVENDISH LawCards®

English Legal System

Second Edition

G000038072

Cavendish
Publishing
Limited

London • Sydney

Second edition first published 1999 by Cavendish Publishing Limited, The Glass House, Wharton Street, London WC1X 9PX, United Kingdom

Telephone: +44 (0) 20 7278 8000

Facsimile: +44 (0) 20 7278 8080

E-mail: info@cavendishpublishing.com

Visit our Home Page on http://www.cavendishpublishing.com

British Library Cataloguing in Publication Data

English legal system – 2nd ed – (Cavendish law cards)

1. Law – England 2. Law – Wales

349.4'2

ISBN 1 85941 506 7

Printed and bound in Great Britain

Contents

1 Sources of law

Common law and equity

Development of the common law

Before the Norman Conquest, there was no unified system of law.

Types of courts

The Norman Conquest

Generally, law is regarded as beginning with the Norman Conquest, which made many changes. There was a strong centralised government headed by the King and advised by his Council (*Curia Regis*).

The common law

A common law was established by the 'general eyre', which eventually created the first national courts. Good local customs were applied promoting certainty and consistency; the doctrine of *stare decisis* was born.

Defects of the common law: rise of equity

Writs were very specific. In common law, if there was no writ, there was no remedy. Money damages were the only remedy. The law favoured the rich and many rights were not recognised. No right of subpoena existed to compel witnesses to give evidence.

The rise of equity

Equity created new rights. New procedures were introduced, for example, the right to subpoena and discovery of documents. The rich nobles resented equity because of the reduction in their incomes. This resulted in the Provisions of Oxford 1258, prohibiting expansion of writs. This statute was later modified after complaints.

Equitable remedies

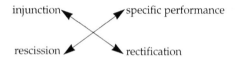

Advantages of equity

Equity was less rigid and formal than the common law, resulting in more flexibility. It was fairer, dealing with cases on their merit. It was described as a 'gloss upon the law'.

Defects of equity

Equity lacked certainty. It varied from chancellor to chancellor. It became overburdened and slow moving.

The Judicature Acts 1873–75

The Judicature Acts resolved the difficulties and reorganised the existing courts, fusing the common law courts and the court of chancery. Both common law and equity decisions could be given in any court.

English and European law

Institutions of the European Community

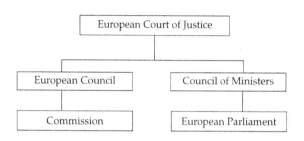

Sources of Community law

Primary sources

Community Treaties

Secondary sources

Regulations, Directives
Decisions

The legislative process

Forms of legislation
Acts of Parliament

The legislative procedure

| First reading | Formal procedure: name of the Bill is read |

| *Second reading* | Main debate on the whole Bill |

| Committee stage, Report stage | Bill is examined in detail and Committee reports back with suggested amendments |

| Third reading | Final vote on the whole Bill |

| House of Lords | Limited power: can suggest amendments |

| Royal Assent | Monarch approves Bill and gives consent |

Types of delegated legislation

Delegated legislation

Promulgated by bodies other than Parliament itself, this type of legislation is necessary for expediency. Sometimes known as subordinate legislation, but is not inferior to other legislation.

Orders in Council

Statutory instruments

Byelaws

Disadvantages of delegated legislation

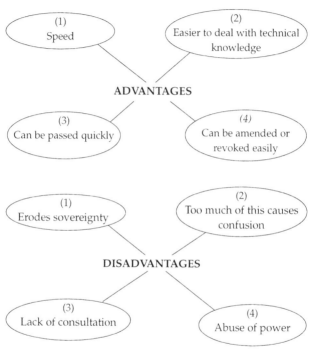

(1)
Speed

(2)
Easier to deal with technical
knowledge

ADVANTAGES

(3)
Can be passed quickly

(4)
Can be amended or
revoked easily

(1)
Erodes sovereignty

(2)
Too much of this causes
confusion

DISADVANTAGES

(3)
Lack of consultation

(4)
Abuse of power

Case law

Created by judges, case law is criticised for its inconsistency and bulk; it is preponderous in nature. Difficulties can arise when determining the law in a particular judgment. However, case law is flexible and can reflect current changes in society.

2 The legal profession

Barristers: training and nature of the work

Barristers are known as the consultant specialists of the legal profession.

Barristers' training

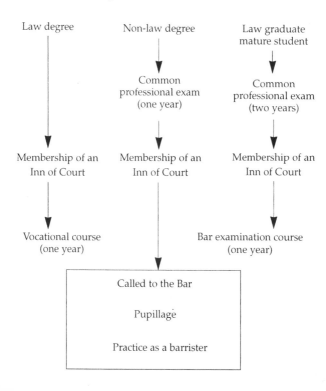

Nature of the work

Barristers generally work in chambers, although it is no longer compulsory for them to do so. They are now permitted to practise alone, working from an office or home. Working from the Bar Library is now no longer necessary. The rule that barristers must deal with clients directly has been modified so that accountants and other professionals can instruct a barrister. Barristers are now allowed to advertise their services in newspapers, a major change introduced under the Courts and Legal Services Act 1990.

The changing Bar and its future

Because of the threat of competition, the Bar has been forced to examine its own working practices to improve services and promote its image. The conduct of the Bar is regulated by a Code of Conduct. One of the main provisions of the new code of conduct is a tightening of the 'cab rank' rule. Barristers are now duty bound to accept legal aid cases. Barristers are also not allowed to discriminate in respect of the type of clients they will represent, so that access to the barrister will be open to all, regardless of sex, race, etc.

According to the latest figures (*Annual Report 1998*, 1999, The General Council of the Bar, London), there were 9,698 barristers in independent practice in England and Wales in 1998, of whom 7,288 were men and 2,410 were women. There were 1,006 Queen's Counsel, of whom 974 were men and 72 women.

Solicitors: training and nature of the work

Solicitors' training

Nature of the work

The main work of a solicitor is very varied. They advise and represent clients, draw up wills, contracts and partnership agreements, do conveyancing, matrimonial work, form companies and deal with accident claims, etc. They are responsible for all the preparatory pre-court work. They are entitled to rights of audience in lower courts and in uncontested cases in the High Court. The Courts and Legal Services Act 1990 has introduced new advocacy rights of audience to the higher courts.

Solicitors and the changing legal profession

Changes in the legal profession have altered their role substantially. The extension of the legal services being offered to other professional bodies has eroded the traditional monopolies which existed for solicitors.

A significant area of development and concern for solicitors at the beginning of the 21st century is the extent to which their monopolies of certain sorts of practice have been eroded. They have already lost their monopoly on conveyancing (although only a solicitor is authorised to give final endorsement to such work if carried out by a licensed conveyancer). Then, in 1999, the Access to Justice Act introduced the provision that the Lord Chancellor will, in future, be able to authorise bodies other than the Law Society to approve of their members carrying out litigation. This, however, should be seen in the wider context of the policy to break down the historical monopolies of both branches of the legal profession. Thus, we can note the growth, since the Courts and Legal Services Act 1990, of solicitors' rights of audience in court and a corresponding anxiety at the Bar when these rights were granted.

CAVENDISH LawCards

The 1999 Act provides that every barrister and every solicitor has a right of audience before every court in relation to all proceedings. The right, however, is not unconditional. In order to exercise it, solicitors and barristers must obey the rules of conduct of the professional bodies and must have met any training requirements that have been prescribed, like the requirement to have completed pupillage in the case of the Bar or to have obtained a higher courts advocacy qualification in the case of solicitors who wish to appear in the higher courts.

Legal services

Other professional bodies

The legal profession has been forced to compete with other bodies in respect of their traditional monopolies. The monopolies enjoyed by the profession were thought to be against the interests of the public using these services. The Administration of Justice Act 1985 ended the monopoly on conveyancing, allowing licensed conveyancers to practise in this area. Similarly, probate work can be undertaken by licensed probate practitioners. Non-lawyers can apply to have rights of audience in the courts. Forcing solicitors to become more competitive has improved the legal services being offered to the public, in terms of the quality of service and price.

Legal executives: role and training

The Institute of Legal Executives

The Institute of Legal Executives (ILEX) was established in 1963 and is the governing body for legal executives. The Institute provides training and a career structure for solicitors' staff. Legal executives play an important role and can be involved in specialised areas, such as probate, trust work, conveyancing, matrimonial, civil or criminal litigation. Employed by solicitors, they can deal comprehensively with the client and manage branch offices. They have no rights of audience, but can appear in front of a judge on uncontested matters.

Training

There is a two part training scheme. Part I involves a broad introduction to key areas of law. In Part II, students study four subjects in more depth. To qualify as a Fellow, a member must be 25 and have a minimum of five years' experience in legal practice.

The Courts and Legal Services Act 1990

Promoting change

Much dissatisfaction had been expressed regarding the high fees the profession charged for conveyancing services. The government had made a commitment to a *laissez faire* doctrine for the provision of legal services. Legal services were to be competitive and orientated towards the consumer. The profession was forced to look at the services it was providing and became more competitive as its traditional monopolies were taken away by other professional bodies offering efficient and cheaper legal services. In 1989, the Lord Chancellor introduced a Green Paper, *The Work and Organisation of the Legal Profession* (Cm 570) reinforcing the governments commitment to a *laissez faire* doctrine for the provision of legal services.

Implementations under the Courts and Legal Services Act 1990

Development of legal services

Section 17 of the 1990 Act provides for the development of legal services in England and Wales. The Act is concerned to regulate and supervise non-solicitors, and ss 34 and 35 set up an Authorised Conveyancing Practitioners' Board. Section 41 introduces a Conveyancing Appeals Tribunal and s 43 sets up a Conveyancing Ombudsman to deal with complaints against authorised practitioners. Section 53 provides for the Council for Licensed Conveyancers to be a recognised body.

Extended rights of audience

Section 27 sets out the guidelines for rights of audience and rights to conduct litigation. Since April 1994, solicitors qualified as barristers, or who sit as part time judges, can use their extended rights in the Crown Court, High Court, Court of Appeal and the House of Lords. The Bar's monopoly has now been broken.

3   The judiciary

The judiciary consists of 12 Lords of Appeal in Ordinary (Law Lords), 35 Lords Justice of Appeal, 96 High Court judges, 539 Circuit judges, 864 Recorders and 337 District judges.

Appointment and tenure

The Act of Settlement 1700 laid down the statutory foundation for the appointment of judges. Judges held office *quamdiu se bene gesserint* (if they were of good behaviour). This gave judges security of tenure and they could be removed only upon address of both Houses of Parliament. However, no English judge has been removed under this procedure. This security of tenure available to the superior judge is not enjoyed by circuit judges or recorders; they can be removed by the Lord Chancellor for misbehaviour or incapacity. From April 1995, posts for circuit judges and district judges must be advertised, applicants being selected by a panel. This move was intended to combat some of the criticisms in respect of the appointment of judges.

The independence of the judiciary

Judges must be completely impartial when applying the law and should not allow any political favour or bias to influence their judgment. The idea of the independence of the judiciary from the State is important to the legal system; protection from removal and the doctrine of judicial immunity reinforces this. Much stress is laid upon the constitutional importance of the independence of judges and accords with Montesquieu's theory of the separation of the powers. To maintain the idea of non-political interference, judges cannot be members of Parliament. However, the Lord Chancellor's position is rather incongruous, having a foot in both camps – being a political appointee and member of the government.

Judicial immunity from civil suit protects superior judges in respect of their activities during the course of judicial office.

Judicial offices

The Lord High Chancellor

↓

Lord Chief Justice

↓

Master of the Rolls

↓

Vice Chancellor

↓

Lords of Appeal in Ordinary

↓

High Court judges

↓

Circuit judges

↓

District judges

Social background of the judiciary

The judiciary is criticised because its members are usually drawn from a very elite social background, mostly from public schools and Oxford or Cambridge universities. They are from upper middle class origins and it is suggested that, because of this and their isolation from life within society, they are out of touch with the moral values of the generation they are trying and sentencing.

Training of judges

Judges receive a training from the Judicial Studies Board. In 1998, there were 2,000 judicial training days (when any one judge is training not sitting); in 1999, the number will be more than 10,000. It will include training judges how not to be rude or offensive in court.

Magistrates

Lay justices

Lay justices sit in magistrates' courts, are part time and are unpaid, receiving only expenses. They try the majority of minor criminal offences; approximately 98% of all criminal offences are processed through the magistrates' court. Lay justices are vital to the legal system as they provide a cheap and quick system of justice. They are appointed by the Lord Chancellor from individuals put forward by local organisations. They must be over 21, not be over 70 and, usually, must live or work in the particular area.

Unlike superior judges, magistrates are not subject to the doctrine of judicial independence; many are local councillors. Though a balance is attempted to ensure that certain groups in the population are represented, many groups are, in fact, excluded. Magistrates are predominantly white, middle class males and this imbalance causes concern. There are not enough women magistrates: research by Baldwin (1976) showed this tendency to be prevalent and the feeling is that magistrates are not a true representation of the community.

Stipendiary magistrates

The word 'magistrate' incorporates the professional stipendiary magistrate, as well as the lay justice of the peace. Stipendiary magistrates are paid, usually barristers or solicitors. They preside over busy magistrates' courts where the use of lay justices would be impracticable; they can preside on their own. The Access to Justice Act 1999 introduces a new name for stipendiary magistrates – District Judge (Magistrates' Court), and re-organises the 91 such magistrates into a single 'bench'.

The justices' clerk

Lay magistrates can only sit if they have a qualified clerk to assist them. He advises the justices as to the law and practice; however, he is not allowed to interfere with their decision. The clerk is salaried, usually a barrister or solicitor.

Judicial reasoning

Case law and judicial precedent

A prominent element of common law systems is the principle of *stare decisis*. It is common to speak today of law being 'judge made'. When deciding a case, judges must look to previous case law decided in similar cases. Judges are bound to decide cases using existing legal principles. The doctrine of judicial precedent depends on the hierarchy of the courts for its operation; courts are bound to follow decisions of higher courts and, usually, previous decisions of its own.

Hierarchy of English courts

Court	Courts bound by it	Courts it must follow
European Court	All courts	None
House of Lords	All English courts	European Court
Court of Appeal	Divisional courts High Court Crown Courts County courts Magistrates' courts	European Court House of Lords
Divisional courts	High Court Crown Courts County courts Magistrates' courts	European Court House of Lords Court of Appeal
High Court	County courts Magistrates' courts	European Court House of Lords Court of Appeal Divisional courts
Crown Courts County courts Magistrates' courts	None	European Court House of Lords Court of Appeal Divisional courts High Court

The House of Lords
Since 1966, the House is no longer bound by its own decisions. All decisions of the House of Lords are binding on all other courts.

Statutory interpretation

It is not an easy task for courts to interpret Acts of Parliament. Problems of construction arise when judges have to use their traditional skills to resolve them. There is no Act of Parliament to guide judges in the interpretation of other Acts, although the Interpretation Act 1978 gives some assistance. Judges can refer to the European Commission's

Three main rules

The Mischief Rule
Rule in *Heydon's Case* (1584) The courts look to the purpose of the Act to fulfil that purpose

The Golden Rule
Supplements the literal rule. Words should be interpreted to give best effect to Parliament's intention

The Literal Rule
Simple words which have obvious everyday meanings should be given that meaning by the court

Maxims of interpretation

Ejusdem generis
categories of words and classes of persons are referred to only if they are in the classification

Expressio unius exclusio alterus
this will exclude other members if a specific member of a class is mentioned

Noscitur a sociis
must read words in the section in this context

explanations when dealing with issues of EC law. As more laws become statute based, interpretation of these statutes is a key role of a judge.

Since the decision in *Pepper v Hart* (1993), a judge can refer to *Hansard* to aid him in interpretation of a statute. However, the rule has its limitation: it can only be used if the statute is ambiguous or if the use of the literal meaning would lead to an absurdity.

Rules of statutory construction
When statutory words are ambiguous, judges can use rules of construction to aid them in determining what it was Parliament had intended.

Intrinsic aids

The title (long or short)	Preamble	Headings

Interpreting EC law
When interpreting EC law, the English courts must interpret the Treaties in line with the European Court of Justice. The importance lies in the actual principles and not with the wording of the decision. Courts do not examine words in detail – they do not apply a strict literal interpretation, but English courts must follow the same principles as the European Court (*HP Bulmer Ltd v J Bollinger SA* (1974)).

4 The criminal courts and court procedure

Magistrates' courts

93% of criminal cases are dealt with by the magistrates' courts. Magistrates try:

- summary offences, tried without a jury; petty motoring offences, theft, common assault, etc;

- indictable offences which are triable summarily at the option of the accused;

- magistrates conduct preliminary investigations of indictable offences to decide if there is a case to answer. If there is, the defendant is committed for trial to the Crown Court.

Committal proceedings

The Royal Commission on Criminal Justice argued that committal proceedings were not as effective as they should be. Old style committals have been abolished by s 44 of the Criminal Justice and Public Order Act 1994 and are now replaced by a new procedure of transfer of trial proceedings.

Now, s 51 of the Crime and Disorder Act 1998 states that, where an adult is charged with an offence triable only on indictment, the court shall send him directly to the Crown Court for trial. Where he is also charged with an either way offence or a summary offence, he may be sent directly to trail for that as well, provided the magistrates believe that it is related to the indictable offence and, in the case of a summary offence, it is punishable with imprisonment or involves obligatory or discretionary disqualification from

driving. This system is being piloted in some courts in 1999
with a view to extension nationally in due course.

Composition of court
Courts exercising criminal jurisdiction

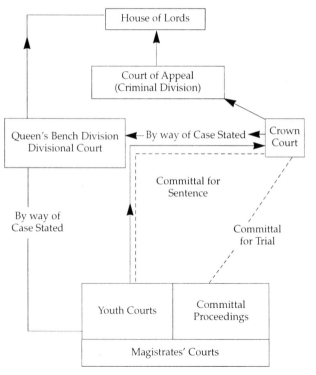

Note: Appeals are indicated thus: ──────────►

Usually, there are between two and seven justices of the peace sitting on the bench; or a stipendiary magistrate.

Jurisdiction

Magistrates have the power to imprison a convicted person for six months and can impose fines up to £5,000, as well as various community service orders. Magistrates can, if they think the offence is sufficiently serious to warrant a longer custodial sentence, commit the defendant to the Crown Court for sentencing.

Crown Court

The Courts Act 1971 introduced the Crown Court. The Crown Court is part of the Supreme Court of Judicature (consisting of the Court of Appeal, the High Court of Justice and the Crown Court). There are three tiers:

- Queen's Bench Division (QBD) judges trying Class 1 offences (murder, treason, etc);

- second tier courts may have QBD judges or circuit judges and try Class 2 offences (rape, manslaughter, etc);

- third tier courts try Class 3 offences, with circuit judges or recorders in charge. Recorders are part time judges appointed on a temporary basis.

High Court

This is structured in three divisions:

- Queen's Bench Division;

- Chancery Division; and

- Family Division.

The Access to Justice Act 1999 – jurisdiction

The Access to Justice Act 1999 establishes the jurisdiction of the High Court to hear cases stated by the Crown Court for an opinion of the High Court. It enables these and certain other applications to the High Court to be listed before a single judge. It provides for the appointment of a Vice President of the Queen's Bench Division. It also prohibits the publication of material likely to identify a child involved in proceedings under the Children Act 1989 before the High Court or a county court; and allows for under 14s to attend criminal trials.

Jurisdiction of single judge of High Court

The Act allows certain applications to be routinely heard by a single judge of the High Court. It does this by removing an obstacle that exists in the current legislation by which the route of appeal for these cases is to the House of Lords, but the Administration of Justice Act 1960 provides that the House of Lords will only hear appeals in these matters from a Divisional Court (that is, more than one judge) of the High Court. The 1999 Act amends the 1960 Act, so that the House of Lords can hear appeals from a single High Court judge. It will then be possible to make rules of court to provide for these cases to be heard by a single judge, while enabling the judge to refer particularly complex cases to a Divisional Court.

The cases in question include:

* appeals by way of case stated in criminal causes and matters;

* appeals from inferior (civil and criminal) courts and tribunals in contempt of court cases;

* criminal applications for habeas corpus.

Another change made by the 1999 Act concerns appeals from the Crown Court for opinion of High Court. The Supreme Court Act 1981 gives the High Court specific powers of disposal over appeals by way of case stated coming from a magistrates' court. However, it does not do the same for cases coming from the Crown Court. The Access to Justice Act 1999 provides a statutory footing for the powers of the High Court to deal with appeals by way of case stated coming from the Crown Court.

Appeals (criminal)

Appeals regarding criminal cases are sent to the Criminal Division of the Court of Appeal. The court hears appeals by the accused on questions of fact, questions of law, the sentence passed on the defendant and appeals by the prosecution on points of law (where an accused has been acquitted). The Criminal Appeal Act 1995 now states that an appeal from the Crown Court against conviction must have leave from the Court of Appeal.

Composition of court
The Lord Chief Justice, Lords Justices of Appeal and *puisne* judges of the QBD.

House of Lords as a Court of Appeal

The Judicial Committee of the House of Lords is the highest Court of Appeal.

Composition of court
The Lord Chancellor, the Lords of Appeal in Ordinary, any other Law Lord who has held high judicial office.

Types of cases

Criminal matters from the Court of Appeal or a Divisional Court of the QBD, if leave to appeal has been granted from the lower court, or from the House itself.

Appeal function of the European Court of Justice

Article 234 (pre-Amsterdam Treaty, Art 177) can render a preliminary ruling if a case in a British court is concerned with the meaning of a particular section of European Community law. The court can then refer the matter to the European Court. Lord Denning laid down rules regarding applications for a preliminary ruling *obiter dicta*:

- if a decision can be reached without a ruling, then there is no need to apply;

- if a similar case has been decided by the European Court, then there is need only to follow the precedent;

- if the point is clear, there is no need for a ruling, just apply the Treaty;

- The facts must be decided first before applying for a ruling.

- all the circumstances need to be taken into consideration – if applying for a ruling will cause delay, for example, or whether the parties wish to apply for a ruling.

The youth court

The youth court will deal with offenders aged between 10 and 17 (Criminal Justice Act 1991), which must be considered in the context of the Children Act 1989. The Children Act 1989 gave statutory recognition to the need to avoid prosecution. Local authorities are required to take reasonable steps to reduce the need to bring criminal proceedings against children and young persons. The Criminal Justice Act 1991 identifies a number of changes, all in line with the welfare principle embodied in the Children Act:

- s 70 renames the juvenile court the 'youth court';

- s 68 extends the jurisdiction so that the youth court and not the magistrates' court will deal with people under 18;

- Pt III gives youth court magistrates new sentencing powers, together with a new scheme of past custody supervision;

- Pt I of the Act applies to offenders of all ages;

- the criteria for passing a custodial sentence are similar to those governing the use of custody for offenders under 21 which were contained in s 1(2) of the Criminal Justice Act 1982. These criteria helped reduce custodial sentences on juvenile offenders between 1980 and 1989.

Section 34 of the Crime and Disorder Act brought 10–14 year olds within the criminal law by abolishing the rebuttable presumption of *doli incapax* for that age range. Now, prosecutions against 10–14 year olds will no longer have to prove that a defendant knew the difference between right and wrong before proceeding to prove the charge in issue.

The youth court will be able to give either a probation order or a supervision order to a 16 or 17 year old. The maximum amount of work which can be imposed in a community service order is 240 hours for offenders aged 16 and 17. Juveniles aged 16 can be compelled to attend an attendance centre for up to 36 hours. The new combination order introduced by s 2 of the 1991 Act will be available for 16 and 17 year olds as well as adults.

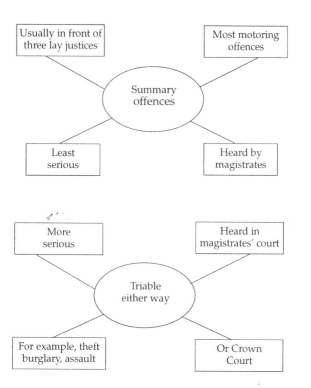

Classification of offences

The Crown Prosecution Service was set up in 1985 as the State's official prosecuting agency. In 1999, it underwent fundamental re-organisation and is now based on 42 regional units which correspond to those of the police services of England and Wales.

In its 1997/98 Annual Report (London: HMSO), the CPS states that, in the year under review, it dealt with more than 1.4 million cases in the magistrates' courts and around 128,000 in the Crown Court. The organisation is clearly under a certain pressure, as only 50.6% of committal papers were delivered to the defence within agreed timescales. The report notes that, in the magistrates' courts, the overall conviction rate was 98.1% (compared with 98.0% in 1996–97). The conviction rate in the Crown Court was 90.6% compared with 90.8% in 1996–97. These figures, though, represent cases which end up in court and they include guilty pleas. The number of discontinuances in both sorts of court is high. Discontinuances occur where witnesses fail to attend or attend and change their evidence. In 1997–98, there were 164,438 cases discontinued by the CPS in the magistrates' courts (12% of all cases brought – the same as the year before) and 8,130 cases not proceeded with in the Crown Court (7.7% of all cases brought, 1,504 more abandoned cases than the year before).

The document *Judicial Statistics 1997* (1998, Lord Chancellor's Department) notes that, of the 91,110 cases being brought to trial at Crown Court in 1997, only 11,510 defendants who pleaded not guilty to all or some the charges against them were convicted by juries.

Police and Magistrates' Courts Act 1994

This Act has increased governmental interference in the police and magistrates' courts service in order to promote more efficiency in the administration of the police and courts. The Act gives new powers to the Home Secretary regarding the appointment of members of police authorities and accountability from chief constables.

Magistrates' courts

Important changes to the magistrates' court system were made by the Access to Justice Act 1999.

The Act contains a range of provisions relating to magistrates and magistrates' courts:

- it provides for various changes to the organisation and management of magistrates' courts;

- it unifies the provincial and metropolitan stipendiary magistrates into a single bench;

- it removes the requirement for magistrates to sit on cases committed to the Crown Court for sentence; and enables the Crown Court, rather than a magistrates' court, to deal with breaches of community sentences imposed by the Crown Court;

- it extends and clarifies the powers of civilians to execute warrants; this is intended to enable this function to be transferred from the police to the magistrates' courts.

The government's objective is to develop a magistrates' court service which is effectively and efficiently managed, at a local level by local people, within a consistent national framework. As part of this programme of reform, the Act includes provisions to:

- reform the organisation and management of the magistrates' courts by:

  › creating more flexible powers to alter the various territorial units that make up the magistrates' court service and to allow summary cases to be heard outside the commission area in which they arose;

- expanding the potential membership of magistrates' courts committees by removing the limit on co-opted members;

- establishing a single authority to manage the magistrates' courts service in London;

- removing the requirement for justices' chief executives to be qualified lawyers and transferring responsibility for certain administrative functions from justices' clerks to justices' chief executives; and

- giving the Lord Chancellor power to require all MCCs to procure common goods and services, where he considers this will lead to more effective or efficient administration;

- unify the provincial and metropolitan stipendiary benches into a single bench of District Judges (Magistrates' Courts), able to sit in any magistrates' court in the country;

• remove the requirement for lay magistrates to sit as judges in the Crown Court on committals for sentence;

• extend and clarify the powers of civilians to execute warrants.

The new powers to change organisational units reflect the government's intention to develop a more coherent geographical structure for the criminal justice system as a whole. Common boundaries should enable the various criminal justice agencies to co-operate more effectively.

The investigation of crime

The normal method of arrest is under a warrant issued by a magistrate or higher judicial officer (s 1 of the Magistrates' Courts Act 1980).

The name of the suspect is unknown or cannot be discerned; or there are reasonable grounds for believing arrest is necessary in order to protect the suspect from:

Causing physical harm to himself or others

Suffering physical injury

Causing unlawful obstruction of the highway

Causing loss or damage to property

Committing public decency offence

Arrestable and serious arrestable offences as defined in ss 24 and 116

Arrest without a warrant

A constable can arrest without warrant if there is reasonable ground for believing that an arrestable offence has been committed or when general arrest provisions exist. Under s 24 of the Police and Criminal Evidence Act (PACE) 1984, the police have wide powers to arrest without warrant.

Arrest for non-arrestable offences

Only the police have this power. This can be done if any of the general arrest conditions under s 25(3) of PACE 1984 are satisfied:

Powers of arrest (s 24)

Section 24 of PACE 1984 defines the powers of arrest:

- anyone may summarily arrest (without warrant) any person who is reasonably suspected of committing an arrestable offence or is actually committing such an offences, or any person who has committed an arrestable offence or is reasonably suspected to have done so;

- the police may also arrest a person who is about to commit an arrestable offence (*Hussein v Chong Fook Kam* (1970)). 'Suspicion' was defined as a state of conjecture where proof is lacking (*James v Chief Constable of South Wales Police Force* (1991)). Under s 116, an arrestable offence could become a serious arrestable offence if there is:

  ɔ serious harm to State security or public order;

  ɔ serious interference with the administration of justice in a particular case;

  ɔ serious injury or death, or substantial gain or loss.

An arrest will be unlawful where the reasons given by the arresting officer point to an offence for which no power of arrest is given (or for which there is only qualified power of arrest) and it is clear that no other reasons were present to the mind of the officer (*Edwards v DPP* (1993)). This principle was confirmed in *Mullady v DPP* (1997). A police officer arrested M for 'obstruction', an offence with the power of arrest only if the defendant's conduct amounted to a breach of the peace (for which there is a common law power of arrest) or if one of the general arrest conditions, as set out in s 25, is satisfied. The police argued that the officer could have arrested M for a breach of the peace and merely gave the wrong reason. The Divisional Court held that the officer had acted unlawfully and that it would be wrong for the justices to go behind the reason given and infer that the reason for the arrest was another lawful reason.

Common law arrest for breach of peace

Under common law, any individual can arrest anyone who is committing a breach of the peace. A constable can arrest anyone who is obstructing him in the execution of his duty and can call upon the general public to assist him, using reasonable force if necessary; there is no need for arrest to be followed by a charge. The person can be released without being able to claim that he has been falsely imprisoned (*Holgate-Mohammed v Duke* (1984)).

The power of the police to enter and deal with a breach of the peace is embodied in a number of cases (*McConnell v Chief Constable of the Greater Manchester Police* (1990); *Howell* (1981); *Lamb v DPP* (1989)).

Arrest procedures

When an arrest is made, the arresting officer must make it clear to the individual that he is being arrested and state the reasons for the arrest. If this is not possible, then the person being arrested should be informed as soon as practicable to do so (s 28 of PACE 1984). If these rules are not observed, it could render the arrest unlawful:

- s 29 of PACE deals with arrests made while the individual is at the police station voluntarily;

- s 30 embodies the general requirement whereby an individual must be taken as soon as possible to a police station after arrest.

Duties of the custody officer

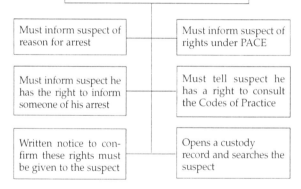

Custody officer is the guardian of the suspect's rights while in custody. He must remain independent from the investigation. However, in practice, this is difficult: *Absolam* (1989)

Must inform suspect of reason for arrest	Must inform suspect of rights under PACE
Must inform suspect he has the right to inform someone of his arrest	Must tell suspect he has a right to consult the Codes of Practice
Written notice to confirm these rights must be given to the suspect	Opens a custody record and searches the suspect

Helping with inquiries

The police do not have the power to detain an individual in order to assist them with their inquiries. The person must be actually arrested (*Lemsatef* (1977)).

Section 29 of PACE states that a person who attends a police station to assist the police in their inquiries has the right to leave at any time, if not arrested by the police. There is no legal duty on the police to point this fact out to the person. It is obviously in the interests of the police to gather as much information as they can before charging the suspect. The protection of a suspect's rights under PACE 1984 does not come into effect until the suspect has been arrested and, therefore, it is in the interests of the arresting officer to delay arrest.

Delay of arrest
Though the police are under no legal duty to inform the suspect of his rights prior to arrest, if it is thought that the delay in arresting the suspect was to deliberately circumvent the protections under PACE, a court may exclude any confession which results from the interview (*Ismail* (1990)).

Booking in
When a police officer detains a suspect, he must be taken as soon as is practicable to a designated police station. Section 36 of PACE provides that the designated station must have a custody officer normally of the rank of sergeant. It is the custody officer who will make the decision whether to detain the suspect.

Searching the suspect
The custody officer searches the suspect and details of the suspect's property are recorded in the custody record. Personal items are usually retained by the suspects (not money or valuables). The custody officer can retain any articles with which he believes the suspect may cause injury to himself or others.

Intimate body searches
A strip search can be carried out if this is necessary. Intimate body searches can be carried out with the permission of an officer at least of the rank of superintendent. Intimate

searches for drugs or harmful objects should be undertaken by a nurse or doctor or, if not practicable, by an officer of the same sex. Section 117 allows the police to use reasonable force to search.

Detention without charge

As seen, it is in the interests of the police to detain a suspect without charge for as long as possible in order to gain further information about the offence committed. The rules governing interviewing of suspects are contained in the Codes of Practice. Meals, refreshment and rest breaks must be given to the suspect during his detention.

Vulnerable suspects

The Codes of Practice state that the police cannot obtain answers to questions by using tricks or oppression and vulnerable suspects must be accorded certain rights. The custody officer must arrange for an 'appropriate adult' to attend if the suspect being interviewed is:

- a juvenile;

- blind;

- mentally handicapped; or

- unable to read.

The suspect can object to the appropriate adult being present (*DPP v Blake* (1989)). If the suspect is mentally handicapped and makes a confession with no 'appropriate adult' present, the confession may be excluded. If the judge admits the confession, he must give a warning to the jury on the danger of convicting on the basis of the confession (*Lamont* (1989)).

Medical treatment

The custody officer must arrange for medical treatment if a suspect requires it. If a doctor deems a suspect unfit to be interviewed, then a further medical examination should be given before the suspect is interviewed. However, failure to obtain a subsequent medical examination will not breach the code in itself (*Trussler* (1988)).

Failure to observe these principles may result in any confession being rendered inadmissible in evidence (*Everett* (1988); *DPP v Blake* (1989)).

Time limits

There are strict time limits on the detention of suspects without charge. An arrested person may not be detained without charge for more than 24 hours unless a serious arrestable offence has been committed. It can be extended to 36 hours by a superintendent, to secure or preserve evidence. If a serious arrestable offence has been committed and the suspect has been detained for 36 hours, the police must bring him before a magistrates' court to extend the time limit to a maximum of 60 hours.

Review periods

There must be regular review periods of the detention of the suspect. If the suspect has not been charged, the review officer must be at least the rank of inspector and the first review should be carried out no later than six hours from detention; then, every nine hours. If the suspect is charged, the custody officer has the responsibility of review.

Delay in exercising suspect's rights

If a suspect is detained in the police station, he has the right to have a friend or relative informed of his arrest. An officer of the rank of superintendent (or acting rank) (*Alladice* (1988)) can delay the exercise of these rights under s 56(1) of PACE if:

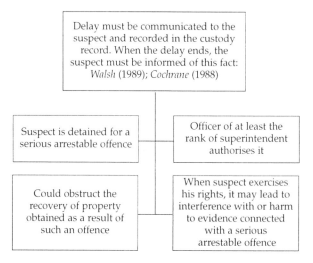

Delay must be communicated to the suspect and recorded in the custody record. When the delay ends, the suspect must be informed of this fact: *Walsh* (1989); *Cochrane* (1988)

Suspect is detained for a serious arrestable offence

Officer of at least the rank of superintendent authorises it

Could obstruct the recovery of property obtained as a result of such an offence

When suspect exercises his rights, it may lead to interference with or harm to evidence connected with a serious arrestable offence

Grounds for delay

- it is not sufficient ground for delay that an accomplice of the suspect was still at large and might be alerted because the arrest was made in a public place in front of people known to the suspect (*Alladice* (1988));

- it was not sufficient ground for delay when the suspect's mother had been informed of the arrest by telephone before the decision to delay access to a solicitor had been made (*Samuel* (1988));

- the police cannot delay access to a solicitor on the ground that access may prejudice police inquiries. Access to a solicitor (s 58 of PACE) is a fundamental safeguard under the Act.

Legal advice at the police station

In *Samuel* (1988), Hodgson LJ commented that the right of access to a solicitor for suspects in police custody is 'one of the most important and fundamental rights of a citizen'.

Section 58(1) of PACE 1984 provides that:

> A person arrested and held in custody ... shall be entitled, if he so requests, to consult a solicitor privately at any time.

A suspect is entitled to consult the duty solicitor if he so wishes. However, the role of the lawyer in the police station has been the subject of much debate. Recent research for the Royal Commission on Criminal Justice by Professor John Baldwin, *The Role of Legal Representatives at Police Stations* (1993), concludes that, on the whole, solicitors are performing badly at police interviews. They tend to adopt a passive role, rather than confront issues on behalf of their client.

Duty solicitor scheme

The duty solicitor arrangements came into force in April 1990. Important changes centred on the duties of the solicitor in responding to a call:

- previously, a duty solicitor on a rota basis had to accept a call from the regional telephone service. Whether he would attend personally at the police station was at his discretion;

- the new arrangements state that a duty solicitor on a rota, or a panel duty solicitor who accepts a call, must provide initial advice to suspects who have asked for the duty solicitor, by talking to them directly on the telephone. The only circumstances where initial telephone advice does not have to be given are:

○ where the solicitor is already at or near to the police station and can provide advice to the suspect immediately;

○ the suspect is not capable of speaking to the solicitor because of intoxication or violent behaviour; in these cases, the solicitor must arrange to provide the initial advice as soon as is practicable.

When the initial advice is provided, the solicitor must attend the suspect at the police station:

If the suspect requests this	If police intend to hold an identification parade
If suspect has been arrested for an offence under s 24 of PACE 1984 and the police wish to question him	If suspect complains of serious maltreatment by the police

Interviews: conduct and control

Absolam (1989) stated:

There was not, in any formal sense, a conventional interview ... but, equally, it was an interview within the provisions of the Code, in that it was a series of questions directed by the police to the suspect, with a view to obtaining admissions on which proceedings could be founded.

There has been much debate as to what actually constitutes 'an interview'. The Report of the Royal Commission on Criminal Justice (1993), para 38, recommends that:

> The definition of an interview in Code C Note for Guidance 11A should be clarified to remove the apparent confusion as to what constitutes an interview for the purposes of the Code.

In *Chung* (1991), the defendant was questioned at his flat. He was arrested and asked to consult his solicitor, but was denied. He was allowed access to his solicitor only after he confessed. His confession was excluded under s 76(2)(b). The evidence was also inadmissible under s 78 (*Absolam* (1989)).

In *Davis* (1990), the statutory procedure under ss 7 and 8 of the Road Traffic Act 1988 with respect to obtaining a breathalyser test from a driver did not constitute an interview for the purposes of Code C. Evidence was wrongly excluded by justices under s 78 of PACE (see, further, *Langiert* (1991); *DPP v McGladrigan* (1991)).

Confession evidence and admissibility

The general principles developed by the courts to govern interviews are:

- suspects must be cautioned before an interview takes place;

- on every new occasion a suspect is exposed to police questioning, he should be given a further caution (*Brown (Kingsley)* (1989));

- the provisions of PACE must be complied with, particularly in respect of meal breaks and rest periods;

- interviews at police stations must be recorded contemporaneously, unless impracticable to do so;

- a record should be made as soon as possible and it must be shown why it was impracticable for the police officer to have made the record at the appropriate time (*Delaney* (1988));

- the record of the interview must be shown to the suspect if the suspect is still in custody at the completion of the record;

- methods employed by the police to obtain evidence must not be used in circumstances which may result in the confession being obtained oppressively, by threats or by bribes.

If there are any doubts about the reliability of police evidence regarding a confession, this can lead to the exclusion of the confession evidence under ss 78 and 76(2)(b).

- *Delaney* (1988):

    failure by the police to make a contemporary record or failure to show it to the suspect, can cast doubt on police evidence, since the confession may have been tampered with in some way;

- *Khan (Hassan)* (1990):

    failure by the police to record interviews causes difficulties for the court when allegations of 'verballing' a suspect are made against the police (*Keenan* (1990));

- *Canale* (1990):

  a confession can be inadmissible if it is obtained by 'oppression' under s 76(2)(A) (*Emmerson* (1991); *Doolan* (1988); *Howard Chung* (1992); *Crampton* (1991); *Goldenberg* (1988)).

Entrapment

There exists no clear authority to determine whether s 78 of PACE allows the exclusion of evidence if an offence is instigated by the police acting as *agents provocateurs* (*Sang* (1979)), even though the courts have disapproved of these methods (*Brannan v Peek* (1948)).

However, s 78 could have prompted some change in *Gill and Ranuana* (1989). Lord Lane stated:

  ... nevertheless, we have no doubt that the speeches in *Sang* and the import of those speeches are matters to be taken into account by a judge when applying the provisions of s 78.

Identification parades

The general principle is that, if the suspect wishes for an identification parade to take place, it must be done unless it would be impracticable to do so. The police must ensure that the parade is fair and any identification of a suspect which is made must be reliable. Breaches of these procedures can lead to the evidence being excluded under s 78 of PACE.

Royal Commission's recommendations

The Commission recommended that:

- if the prosecution evidence is deemed unsafe or unsatisfactory, the judge should be able to stop the case;

- if a confession has been made by the suspect away from the police station, the suspect should be presented with it at the beginning of the first tape recorded interview made at the police station;

- where confession evidence is involved in a case, a judicial warning should be issued.

Criminal Evidence (Northern Ireland) Order 1988

The right to silence in Northern Ireland has been abolished since 1988. It is possible for a court to draw inferences from a defendant's silence at the police station and from him failing to account for his presence at a particular place; or from marks or items found on the defendant which may link him to a crime.

It is further proposed that judges should comment to the jury on a refusal to take the oath or answer questions.

Bail

The question of bail can arise at the police station and again when the accused appears before the court. Bail is defined as:

> The release of a person subject to a duty to surrender to custody at a particular time and place.

Arrest under warrant

If a person has been arrested by warrant, the warrant will usually have provisions included as to whether bail should be granted. The decision is made by the magistrate who issues the warrant.

Arrest not under warrant

If arrest is not under warrant, the police must act in accordance with the provisions contained in PACE.

Under PACE, the custody officer is responsible for deciding whether to continue the detention of a suspect who has not been charged. A person who has been charged must be released unless:

- the police cannot discover the person's name and address or believe that the information given is false;

- the police reasonably believe that detention is necessary for the person's protection or to prevent the person causing harm to someone else or interfering with property; or

- the police reasonably believe that the person will 'jump bail', interfere with witnesses or otherwise obstruct the course of justice.

Bail from court

The granting of bail from court is governed by the Bail Act 1976. Section 4 governs the accused's right to bail. Section 4 gives a right to bail in those cases which do not come within Sched 1 of the Bail Act.

The exceptions to bail are classed in two lists:

- the first list will apply if the defendant is charged with an offence which carries a possible custodial sentence;

- the second list applies if the offence is one which does not carry a custodial sentence.

If it is an imprisonable offence, the court does not have to grant bail if it believes that the defendant may:

| Fail to surrender to custody | Commit an offence while out on bail | Interfere with witnesses or otherwise obstruct the course of justice |

The Criminal Justice and Public Order Act 1994 restricts the granting of bail if the defendant commits another offence while already out on bail.

Appeal against refusal to grant bail

An accused person can appeal to the High Court against a magistrates' decision not to grant bail. An accused person not granted bail can also appeal to the Crown Court, which can grant bail if:

- the magistrates have remanded the defendant in custody after a full bail application has been made;

- if the magistrates have committed the defendant to the Crown Court for trial or sentence; or

- if the magistrates have convicted the accused and refused him bail pending appeal to the Crown Court.

Stop and search

The police powers regarding search of an individual are contained in the Police and Criminal Evidence Act 1984 and the Home Office Codes of Practice.

Under s 1 of PACE, a police officer can stop, detain and search any person that he reasonably suspects may be carrying stolen or prohibited items and seize them. Articles would include offensive weapons; and articles made and adapted for use in connection with an offence, such as burglary; theft; taking of a motor vehicle; or obtaining property by deception.

PACE concentrates the main powers of the police in respect of stop and search, but there are other statutes which exist before and after PACE which allow the police this power:

• Misuse of Drugs Act 1971;

• Firearms Act 1968;

• Aviation Security Act 1982;

• Crossbows Act 1987;

• Prevention of Terrorism (Temporary Provisions) Act 1989.

Section 2 of PACE provides safeguards for the suspect and indicates the extent to which a police officer can search a suspect in a public place. Section 117 allows a police officer to use reasonable force in the exercise of his powers.

Under s 163 of the Road Traffic Act 1988, a police officer has the power to stop any motor vehicle.

Powers under s 60 of the Criminal Justice and Public Order Act 1994

Section 60 of the CJPOA 1994 created new stop and search powers in anticipation of violence. The powers must be authorised by a senior officer and must be limited to where there is a fear of an outbreak of violence. The authorising officer must reasonably believe that it is 'expedient' to give an authorisation in order to prevent the occurrence of incidents of serious violence. Thus, the authorisation need not be the only way in which such serious incidents may be prevented. Various policing factors may have to be balanced, including the ability of the police force to remain effective and efficient if it were to use other methods.

The scope of s 60 of the CJPOA 1994 and police powers to stop and search are being incrementally extended through various Acts of Parliament. They include the following: s 8 of the Knives Act 1997 amended s 60 to allow *initial* authorisations by an inspector or above, thus obviating the need for an officer of at least the rank of superintendent; s 60(1)(b) extends the criteria under which an authorising officer may invoke this power to include reasonable belief that incidents involving serious violence may take place or that such instruments of weapons are being carried in a particular area; and s 60(3) provides that authorisations may be extended up to 24 hours, instead of six, although only an officer of the rank of superintendent or above may do this. A new sub-section, sub-s 11A, was inserted under s 60 by s 8 of the 1997 Knives Act and states that: '... for the purposes of this section, a person carries a dangerous instrument or an offensive weapon if he has it in his possession.' These amendments are intended to deal with anticipated violence in situations where gangs or persons may be 'tooled-up' and travelling through various police areas en route to an intended scene of confrontation. Thus, the power may be invoked, even where it is believed that the actual anticipated violence may occur in another police jurisdiction, for example, by football hooligans travelling to and from matches.

Further amendments to s 60 have recently been made under the Crime and Disorder Act (CDA) 1998. This is mainly to deal with the problem of troublemakers deliberately wearing facial coverings to conceal their identities, especially when the police are using CCTV cameras.

Section 81 of the CJPOA 1994

Section 81 creates a new power of stop and search of persons and vehicles where it is expedient to do so to prevent certain acts of terrorism. Any officer of or above the rank of commander or assistant chief constable may authorise a stop and search where 'it appears to him to be expedient to do so' in order to prevent acts of terrorism connected with Northern Ireland, or international terrorism.

The Code of Practice (A) for the exercise of statutory powers of stop and search

In view of the wide powers vested in the police in the exercise of stop and search, Code A was revised to reflect the new legislation and to clarify how searches under stop and search powers are to be conducted. The revised Code came into effect in 1999 and supersedes the edition of Code A which came into effect in 1997.

Code (1AA) restates the guidance under the previous edition and emphasises:

> It is important to ensure that the powers of stop and search are used responsibly by those who exercise them and those who authorise their use. It is also particularly important to ensure that any person searched is treated courteously and considerately.

Code A states, in relation to the ability of an officer to search a person in the street with his consent, where no search power exists, that:

> In these circumstances, an officer should always make it clear that he is seeking the consent of the person concerned to the search being carried out, by telling the person that he need not consent and that without his consent he will not be searched.

Entry, search and seizure

Section 8 of PACE provides for a general power for magistrates to issue search warrants to the police where there are reasonable grounds for believing that a 'serious arrestable offence' has been committed. The police must have reasonable grounds to suspect that admissible evidence in connection with the offence will be found on the premises and that:

• it is not reasonably practicable to contact any person who could give permission to enter the premises;

• such a person has unreasonably refused to allow the police to enter the premises or hand over the evidence;

• evidence would be hidden, removed or destroyed if the police sought access without a warrant.

Certain articles, such as articles which are subject to legal privilege (that is, between a client and his solicitor), cannot be seized under a warrant. Excluded material includes personal records, such as medical records, specimens for medical purposes and certain journalistic material held in confidence.

In *Central Criminal Court ex p AJD Holdings* (1992), the court stressed that, when police officers request a warrant, they should be clear what evidence it is hoped a search will reveal; further, the application should make it clear how the material relates to the crime which is under investigation.

In *Billericay Justices and Dobbyn ex p Harris Coaches* (1991), a police officer had the power to require the production of documents in pursuance of s 99 of the Transport Act 1968. The officer had, instead, chosen to proceed under the powers in ss 8 and 15 of PACE. The Divisional Court refused the application for judicial review of the magistrates' decision to issue a search warrant.

A search under a warrant 'may only be a search to the extent required for the purpose of which the warrant was issued' (s 16(8)). In *Chief Constable of the Warwickshire Constabulary ex p Fitzpatrick* (1998), the Divisional Court disapproved of the police practice of using a warrant phrased in broad terms to seize every possible item that could broadly fall within those terms. They should ensure both that the material seized falls within the terms of the warrant and, because such a warrant is granted to search for material of evidential value, that there are reasonable grounds for believing so and to be likely to be of substantial value in the investigation. In this case, in relation to one of the warrants, the police officers went on a 'fishing expedition' and seized a large selection of documents not, on their face, related to the offence under investigation. In doing so, they exceeded the ambit of the warrant.

Entry and search without a warrant
Section 18 of PACE 1984 provides the police with the power to enter and search. These provisions relate to entry and search after the arrest for an arrestable offence of a person who occupies or controls the premises, so that further evidence connected with the offence may be obtained. Section 32 allows the police to enter and search any premises if a suspect is arrested away from the police station and was at the premises on or prior to the arrest, in order to search for evidence of the offence committed.

Where evidence of entry and search after arrest is admitted, it is a question for the jury, not the judge, whether the actual purpose of the police officer's search was to search for such evidence. In *Beckford* (1991), confirmation was given by the

Court of Appeal that, under s 32, the police can enter and search premises if the defendant had been in those premises shortly before arrest. The officer's credibility in respect of the search could be tested by the reasons given for the search.

Adverse inference from silence

Following the enactment of the CJPOA 1994, there has been a steady stream of case law as to correct judicial practice when directing the jury about the drawing of adverse inferences under ss 34 and 35.

In *R v Cowan* (1995), the Court of Appeal considered what should be said in the summing up if the defendant decides not to testify. The jury must be directed that (as provided by s 38(3) of the CJPOA 1994) an inference from failure to give evidence could not, on its own, prove guilty. The jury had to be satisfied (on the basis of the evidence called by the prosecution) that the prosecution had established a case to answer before inferences could be drawn from the accused's silence. The jury could only draw an adverse inference from the accused's silence if it concluded that the silence could only be sensibly attributed to the accused having no answer to the charge or none that could stand up to cross-examination.

The difficult issue as to correct judicial practice when the accused remains silent during interview on the advice of his solicitor was considered in *R v Condron* (1997) and *R v Argent* (1997). These cases make it clear that such advice was only one factor to be taken into consideration, along with all the other circumstances, in any jury determination as to whether adverse inferences could be drawn from a 'no comment' interview. In *Condron*, the Court of Appeal considered the guidelines set out in *Cowan* (above) and concluded that they were equally applicable to failure to answer questions (s 34) and failure to testify (s 35). The Court of Appeal approved the Judicial Studies Board specimen direction which states:

> If he failed to mention when he was questioned [a fact which he relied on in his defence], decide whether, in the circumstances which existed at the time, it was a fact he could have reasonably be expected then to mention.

The law is that as a juror you may draw such inferences as appear proper from the defendant's failure to mention something at that time. You do not have to hold it against him. It is for a juror to decide whether it is proper to do so.

It is also desirable to direct the jury that if, despite any evidence relied upon to explain the failure (to answer questions) or in the absence of such evidence, they concluded that the failure could only sensibly be attributed to the accused having fabricated the evidence subsequently, they might draw an adverse inference.

5 The civil process

Key differences in civil and criminal law

Public law
This includes criminal law, constitutional and administrative law. Public law is concerned with the interaction between an individual and the rest of the community.

Private law
This includes tort, contract and divorce law. Private law concerns the interaction between individuals in that community, inasmuch as they do not concern the community as a whole.

It is possible to be both liable in public and private law.

Criminal law is concerned with conduct of which the State disapproves and will punish the wrongdoer, seeking to deter others from similar behaviour.

Civil law has a complementary function. When a dispute arises between two individuals, rules of civil law are applied to determine which individual is in the right. The party in the wrong must then compensate the other for any loss or damage.

The object of the criminal law is, therefore, punitive; the object of the civil law is to compensate the person wronged.

Separate court systems

There are separate systems of courts dealing with criminal and civil cases.

Criminal cases

A criminal prosecution is usually brought by the Crown Prosecution Service, established by s 1 of the Prosecution of Offences Act 1985. The Crown Prosecution Service works independently from the police: *they* take the decision to prosecute, not police officers. Under s 6 of the Prosecution of Offences Act 1985, a private individual can institute a prosecution.

Laying an information
A prosecution can be started by laying an information – either written or oral; or by charging a person with an offence, which is contained in a charge sheet.

The magistrates' court
Magistrates deal with a large volume of civil cases, in particular with family matters. They deal with issues such as:

- judicial separation;

- maintenance payments;

- affiliation orders;

- guardianship of minors;

- adoption orders;

- case orders.

They also have many administrative tasks, such as issuing and renewing licences, dealing with community charge enforcements and recovery of certain civil debts. The Children Act 1989 has widened the jurisdiction of the magistrates in respect of child law and jurisdiction under the youth court (previously the juvenile court) for juveniles under 17 years of age.

Courts exercising civil jurisdiction

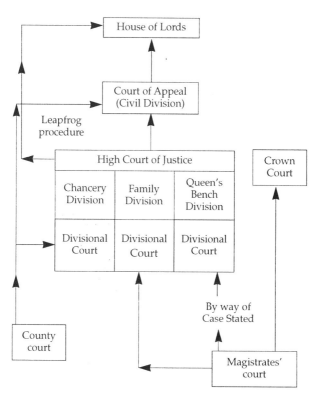

Note: Appeals are indicated thus ⟶

County courts

Established in 1846, county courts provide a cheap system of local justice staffed by circuit judges and district judges.

The High Court

The High Court consists of:

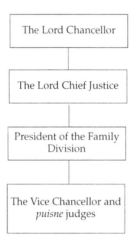

The High Court is split into three basic divisions, each of which is further divided. Any *puisne* judge can deal with any High Court matter, but they tend to specialise.

The Chancery Division

First instance jurisdiction consists of:

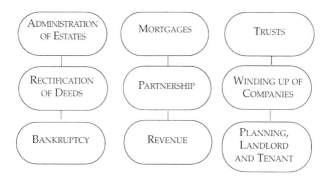

On occasions, other cases are dealt with by other courts, for example:

The courts' appellate jurisdiction hears appeals from decisions of the Inland Revenue Commissioners, and appeals on bankruptcy and land registration cases from the county courts.

The Family Division
Created by the Administration of Justice Act 1970. First instance jurisdiction covers:

* family matters (including all cases concerning marriage – its validity and termination; legitimacy; wardship; adoption; guardianship, custodianship; and family property disputes);

- all issues concerning proceedings under the Children Act 1989; proceedings under the Domestic Violence and Matrimonial Proceedings Act 1976; and s 30 of the Human Fertilisation and Embryology Act 1990.

The court's appellate jurisdiction hears appeals from:

- county courts;
- magistrates' courts; and
- Crown Courts.

The Queen's Bench Division

Largest of the three divisions. Presided over by the Lord Chief Justice. First instance jurisdiction consists of:

- contract actions;
- tort actions.

The division also includes the Admiralty Court dealing, with claims for injury or loss through collisions at sea.

Also includes the Commercial Court, dealing with claims for insurance, banking, agency and negotiable instruments.

The appellate jurisdiction of the High Court is as follows:
- single judge can hear appeals from certain tribunals, and from commercial arbitrators, particularly on points of law;
- Divisional Court of two judges has a certain civil appeal function, for example, from the Solicitor's Disciplinary Tribunal;
- also hears appeals from magistrates' court, which have been to the Crown Court for appeal or sentence, by way of a 'case stated';

- it oversees the activities of all the inferior courts. Can issue three types of prerogative orders and one prerogative unit: mandamus; certiorari; prohibition; habeas corpus.

The House of Lords

- Supreme court of appeal for civil cases in Great Britain and Northern Ireland.

- Appeal to the House of Lords requires leave of the Court of Appeal or, in certain cases, from the High Court or Divisional Court, for leapfrog appeal under the provisions of the Administration of Justice Act.

- Appeals to the House are generally only permitted if there is a point of law of general public importance.

- Appeal committees consist of three Law Lords who report their recommendations to the Appellate Committee.

Judicial Committee of the Privy Council

The Committee hears appeals from Ecclesiastical Courts and certain professional tribunals. Members of the Committee consist of:

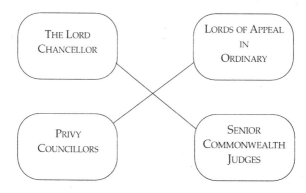

THE LORD CHANCELLOR

LORDS OF APPEAL IN ORDINARY

PRIVY COUNCILLORS

SENIOR COMMONWEALTH JUDGES

European Court of Human Rights

If there is an issue in a case concerning the interpretation of community law, the court must refer the case to the European Court for a ruling (Art 234 of the EC Treaty, formerly Art 177).

In England, if a question of interpretation or validity arises the European Court is supreme (*HP Bulmer Ltd v J Bollinger SA* (1974)).

Organisation of civil courts

There have been many changes in the organisation of civil courts following the recommendations of the Civil Justice Review, initiated in 1985, to speed up the process and improve access to justice.

The Civil Justice Review was concerned to meet the public's criticisms that justice was too slow, inaccessible, very expensive, and extremely complex in its process.

Reform of civil litigation

In February 1985, the then Lord Chancellor, Lord Hailsham, began a review into the machinery of civil justice. The Review was undertaken by the Lord Chancellor's Department under the supervision of an advisory committee chaired by Sir Maurice Hodgson. The review centred on five consultative papers concerning civil litigation:

- personal injury;
- small claims;
- Commercial Court;
- debt enforcement;
- housing.

The final report was published in 1988. Its findings were implemented in the Courts and Legal Services Act 1990.

There has been criticism of the controversial redistribution of court business. The Civil Justice Review had concluded that too many personal injury cases were going through the High Court, cases which were in fact straightforward, and there was no need to take up valuable High Court time. Only 36% of awards at trial and 14% of settlements in the High Court were for sums exceeding £20,000. The biggest problem was the delay in the High Court, litigants waiting up to five years or more. The High Court was to be reserved for public law and specialised cases.

Stephen Sedley QC in 'Improving civil justice' (1990) *Civil Justice Quarterly* stated that:

> ... these measures were to allow for a 'judicial fast track' for public law, particularly commercial cases, at the expense of issues arising from things like accidents at work or on the road, wrongful arrests, contracts of employment or tenancies and housing conditions – in other words, individuals' problems.

The Woolf reforms 1999

When Lord Woolf began his examination of the civil law process, the problems facing those who used the system were many and varied. His Interim Report published in June 1995 identified these problems. He noted, for example, that:

> ... the key problems facing civil justice today are cost, delay and complexity. These three are interrelated and stem from the uncontrolled nature of the litigation process. In particular, there

is no clear judicial responsibility for managing individual cases or for the overall administration of the civil courts. Just as the problems are interrelated, so too the solutions, which, I propose, are interdependent. In many instances, the failure of previous attempts to address the problem stems not from the solutions proposed but from their partial rather than their complete implementation (*Access to Justice*, Interim Report of Lord Woolf, 1995, London).

In the system that Lord Woolf examined, the main responsibility for the initiation and conduct of proceedings rested with the parties to each individual case, and it was normally the plaintiff (now claimant) who set the pace. Thus, Lord Woolf also noted:

> Without effect judicial control, the adversarial process is likely to encourage an adversarial cultural and to degenerate into an environment in which the litigation process is too often seen as a battlefield where no rules apply. In this environment, questions of expense, delay, compromise and fairness have only a low priority. The consequence is that the expense is often excessive, disproportionate and unpredictable; and delay is frequently unreasonable.

The new civil process

The new Civil Procedure Rules 1998 (CPR) will be the same for the county court and the High Court. They apply to all cases except (Pt 2) to insolvency proceedings, family proceedings, and non-contentious probate proceedings. The vocabulary will be more user-friendly, so, for example, what used to be called a 'writ' will be a 'claim form' and a *guardian ad litem* will be a 'litigator's friend'.

Although, in some ways, all the fuss about the new CPR being so far reaching creates the impression that the future will see a sharp rise in litigation, the truth may be different. It seems likely that a fall off in litigation in the 1990s will continue. Queen's Bench Division writs were down from 50,295 in 1993/94 to 22,483 in 1997/98, and county court summonses from 2,577,704 to 1,959,958. During the same period, the number of district judges increased from 289 to 337.

The overriding objective

The overriding objective of the new Civil Procedure Rules (CPR) is to enable the court to deal justly with cases. The first rule reads:

> 1.1(1) These rules are a new procedural code with the overriding objective of enabling the court to deal with cases justly.

This objective will include ensuring that the parties are on an equal footing, and saving expense. When exercising any discretion given by the CPR, the court must, according to r 1.2, have regard to the overriding objective, and a checklist of factors, including the amount of money involved, the complexity of the issue, the parties' financial positions, how the case can be dealt with expeditiously and by allotting an appropriate share of the court's resources while taking into account the needs of others.

Following the Civil Procedure Act 1997, the changes are effected through the new Civil Procedure Rules 1998. These have been supplemented by new practice directions and pre-action protocols. The principal parts of all of these new rules and guidelines are examined below. Thus, 'r 4.1' refers to r 4.1 of the Civil Procedure Rules.

There are three main aspects to the reforms:

(1)   Judicial case management

The judge will become a case manager in the new regime. He or she will be centre stage for the whole action. Previously, lawyers from either side were permitted to wrangle almost endlessly with each other about who should disclose what information and documents to whom and at what stage. Now, the judge is under an obligation to 'actively' manage cases. This includes:

- encouraging parties to co-operate with each other;

- identifying issues in the dispute at an early stage;

- disposing of summary issues which do not need full investigation;

- helping the parties to settle the whole or part of the case;

- fixing timetables for the case hearing and controlling the progress of the case;

- considering whether the benefits of a particular way of hearing the dispute justify its costs.

If the parties refuse to comply with the new rules, the practice directions or the protocols, the judge will be able to exercise disciplinary powers. These include:

- using 'Orders for Costs' against parties (that is, refusing to allow the lawyers who have violated the rules to recover their costs from their client or the other side of the dispute);

- 'unless' orders;

- striking-out;

- refusal to grant extensions of time;

- refusal to allow documents not previously disclosed to the court and the other side to be relied upon.

One of the greatest changes, however, will concern the spirit of the law. The new style of procedure which is intended to be brisk will be of paramount importance. The courts will become allergic to delay or any of the old, ponderous, long-winded techniques previously used by many lawyers.

(2) Pre-action protocols

Part of the problem in the past has arisen from the fact that the courts can only start to exercise control over the progress of a case, and the way it is handled, once proceedings have been issued. Before that stage, lawyers were at liberty to take inordinate time to do things related to the case, to write to lawyers on the other side to the dispute and so forth. Now, a mechanism allows new pre-action requirements to be enforced. Two protocols have been drawn up, to apply in the largest areas of litigation: clinical negligence (including actions against doctors, nurses, dentists, hospitals, health authorities, etc); and personal injury (road accidents, work accidents, etc).

The object of the protocols is:

- to encourage greater contact between the parties at the earliest opportunity;

- to encourage a better exchange of information;

- to encourage better pre-action investigation;

- to put parties in a position to settle cases fairly and early; and

- to reduce the need for the case going all the way to court.

(3)   Alternatives to going to court

Rule 4.1 requires the court as a part of its 'active case management' to encourage and facilitate the use of alternative dispute resolution (ADR), and r 26.4 allows the court to stay proceedings (that is, halt them) to allow the parties to go to ADR either where the parties themselves request it or where the court 'of its own initiative' considers it appropriate.

At the heart of the new system is the allocation of cases to a 'track' according to their complexity and value.

The small claims track

There is no longer any 'automatic reference' to the small claims track. Claims are allocated to this track in exactly the same way as to the fast or multi-tracks. The concept of an *arbitration*, therefore, disappears and is replaced by a *small claims hearing*. Aspects of the old small claims procedure which are retained, include their informality, the interventionist approach adopted by the judiciary, the limited costs regime and the limited grounds for appeal (misconduct of the district judge or an error of law made by the court).

Changes to the handling of small claims are:

- *jurisdiction of up to £5,000* (with the exception of claims for personal injury where the damages sought must be no more than £ 1,000 and for housing disrepair where the claim for repairs and other work and any other claim for damages are both under £ 1,000);

- *paper adjudication, if parties consent* – where a judge thinks that paper adjudication may be appropriate, parties will be asked to say whether or not they have any objections within a given time period. If a party does object, the matter will be given a hearing in the normal way;

- *parties need not attend the hearing* – a party not wishing to attend a hearing will be able to give the court and the other party, or parties, written notice that they will not be attending. The notice must be filed with the court seven days before the start of the hearing. This will guarantee that the court will take into account any written evidence that party has sent to the court. A consequence of this is that the judge must give reasons for the decision reached which will be included in the judgement.

- *the introduction of tailored directions* – to be given for some of the most common small claims, for example, spoiled holidays, or wedding videos, road traffic accidents, building disputes.

Parties can consent to use the small claims track even if the value of their claim exceeds the normal value for that track, but subject to the court's approval. The limited cost regime will not apply to these claims. But costs will be limited to the costs that might have been awarded if the claim had been dealt with in the fast track. Parties will also be restricted to a maximum one day hearing.

The fast track
In accordance with one of the main principles of the Woolf reforms, the purpose of the fast track is to provide a streamlined procedure for the handling of moderately-valued cases – *those with a value of more than £5,000 but less than £15,000* – in a way which will ensure that the costs

remain proportionate to the amount in dispute. The features of the procedure which aim to achieve this are:

- standard directions for trial preparation which avoid complex procedures and multiple experts, with minimum case management intervention by the court;

- a limited period between directions and the start of the trial, or trial period, of around 30 weeks;

- a maximum of one day (five hours) for trial;

- trial period must not exceed three weeks and parties must be given 21 days' notice of the date fixed for trial;

- normally, no oral expert evidence to be given at trial; and fixed costs allowed for the trial which vary depending on the level of advocate.

Directions given to the parties by the judge will normally include a date by which parties must file a listing questionnaire. As with allocation questionnaires, the procedural judge may impose a sanction where a listing questionnaire is not returned by the due date. Listing questionnaires will include information about witnesses, confirm the time needed for trial, parties' availability and the level of advocate for the trial.

The multi-track

The multi-track is intended to provide a flexible regime for the handling of the higher value, more complex claims, that is, those with a *value of over £15,000*.

This track does not provide any standard procedure, such as those for small claims or claims in the fast track. Instead, it offers a range of case management tools – *standard directions, case management conferences and pre trial reviews* – which can

CAVENDISH LAWCARDS

be used in a 'mix and match' way – to suit the needs of individual cases. Whichever of these is used to manage the case, the principle of setting a date for trial, or a trial period at the earliest possible time, no matter that it is some way away, will remain paramount.

Where a trial period is given for a multi-track case, this will be one week. Parties will be told initially that their trial will begin on a day within the given week. The rules and practice direction do not set any time period for giving notice to the parties of the date fixed for trial.

Experts

New rules place a clear duty on the court to ensure that 'expert evidence is restricted to that which is reasonably required to resolve the proceedings'. That is to say, expert evidence will only be allowed either by way of written report, or orally, where the court gives permission. Equally important is the rules' statement about experts' duties. They state that it is the clear duty of experts to help the *court* on matters within their expertise, bearing in mind that this duty overrides any obligation to the person from whom they have received instructions or by whom they are paid.

There will be greater emphasis in the future on using the opinion of a single expert. Experts will only be called to give oral evidence at a trial or hearing if the court gives permission. Experts' written reports must contain a statement that they understand and have complied with their duty to the court. Instructions to experts will no longer be privileged and their substance, whether written or oral, must be set out in the expert's report. Thus, either side can insist, through the court, on seeing how the other side phrased its request to an expert.

Criticism of the new reforms

Professor Michael Zander QC has made substantial criticism of the new civil procedure reforms.

At the heart of the Woolf reforms is the mechanism of 'judicial case management'. Looking at the results of an American study about how the system operates in the United States, Zander raises serious questions about whether the Woolf reforms would be subject to similar problems.

The major official study that Zander examined was published by the Institute of Civil Justice at the Rand Corporation in California. The study was based on 10,000 cases in Federal Courts drawn from 16 States. It appears that a range of judicial case management techniques introduced in America had little effect on the time it took to deal with cases, litigation costs, and lawyer satisfaction. There was evidence that early judicial case management is associated with significantly increased costs to litigants because lawyer work increases in such circumstances.

The Rand Report explains that case management tends to increase rather than reduce costs because it generates more work by lawyer. Zander notes that lawyer work may increase as a result of earlier management because lawyers need to respond to a courts management; for example, talking to the litigant and to the other lawyers in advance of a conference with the judge, travelling and spending time at the court house, meeting with the judge and updating the file after conference.

Professor Zander has taken the view that the reasons for delay in civil legal process are not primarily to do with the adversarial nature of civil litigation. The only serious empirical study of the reasons for delay, argues Zander, is

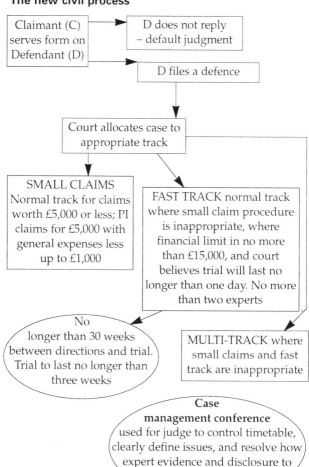

The new civil process

Claimant (C) serves form on Defendant (D) → D does not reply – default judgment

→ D files a defence

Court allocates case to appropriate track

SMALL CLAIMS Normal track for claims worth £5,000 or less; PI claims for £5,000 with general expenses less up to £1,000

FAST TRACK normal track where small claim procedure is inappropriate, where financial limit in no more than £15,000, and court believes trial will last no longer than one day. No more than two experts

No longer than 30 weeks between directions and trial. Trial to last no longer than three weeks

MULTI-TRACK where small claims and fast track are inappropriate

Case management conference used for judge to control timetable, clearly define issues, and resolve how expert evidence and disclosure to be dealt with

that done by KPMG Peat Marwick for the Lord Chancellor's Department in 1994. The KPMG report identified seven causes of delay:

- the nature of the case;
- delay caused by the parties;
- delay caused by their representatives;
- external factors, such as the difficulty of getting experts' reports;
- the judiciary;
- court procedures; and
- court administration.

How the lawyers play the adversary game was not one of these factors. KPMG considered the relative important of the seven factors and found that the two factors that gave rise to the most significant delay were, first, delay caused by lawyers, mainly due to pressure of work and inexperience or inefficiency in the handling of the case by the parties' solicitors, and, secondly, the time taken to obtain medical or other expert reports.

6 Tribunals, inquiries and arbitration

Reasons for their creation

There has grown up over the years a network of administrative tribunals dealing with specific areas of specialism. This has been the consequence of increased State interference into social and economic fields.

Because of the technical and specialised nature of these disputes it is thought that the ordinary courts are ill-equipped to deal with them. The procedure of the ordinary courts is slow and administrative decisions need to be made quickly for efficiency. Delay can cause a claimant severe financial hardship in some cases, and therefore tribunals are favoured over the formal procedures of the courts which are often very expensive.

Administrative tribunals

The workload of the courts is relieved by a large number of administrative tribunals. Tribunals deal with a wide area:

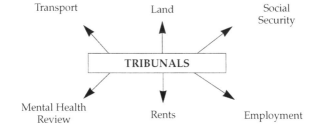

and many more. As society has progressed, certain areas have developed in which complicated disputes concerning technical matters can arise. These disputes are more often than not between private individuals and government departments, hence the term 'administrative tribunals'.

The Tribunals and Inquiries Acts

Tribunals and Inquiries Acts 1958; 1971; 1992.

The Council on Tribunals was established in 1958 and provides general guidance to administrative tribunals. Members are appointed by the Lord Chancellor.

Compensation of tribunals

Tribunals normally consist of a panel of lay members with a chairman who has some legal knowledge. Lack of legal knowledge is not viewed as a drawback, because what is necessary is a cheap, swift, informal method of resolving disputes, and in technical areas cases heard by an expert in that field is more desirable than legal knowledge.

Under the Trade Union Reform and Employment Rights Act 1993, the tribunal chairman will be able to sit alone to hear certain types of cases.

Statutory tribunals

Social security/welfare

An individual has a right to appeal to the Social Security Appeal Tribunal if their application is rejected. The tribunal consists of three members, a chairman who is legally trained, and two lay members. Further appeal lies to the Social Security Commissioners, and further to the Court of Appeal on a question of law.

Tribunals dealing with revenue
These tribunals hear appeals against taxation and VAT assessments. A recently established tribunal, the Valuation and Council Tax Tribunal, deals with appeals against the council tax.

Lands tribunals
There are a number of tribunals which deal with issues relating to land, for example, against compulsory purchase. The lands tribunal is an important tribunal with status similar to the High Court.

Tribunals dealing with transportation
The transport tribunal deals with issues such as appeals over road haulage licences.

Employment tribunals
The main role of these tribunals is to deal with issues relating to employment, for example, discrimination in employment, unfair dismissal, redundancy claims and issues related to health and safety at work. The Industrial Tribunals Act 1996 has consolidated the existing primary legislation in this area.

Mental health review tribunals
These tribunals generally consist of members of the medical profession deciding issues related to matters under the Mental Health Act 1983.

Domestic tribunals
These relate to matters of private rather than public concern and can be set up by legalisation. Examples of domestic tribunals are committees established to discipline their members, for example, barristers are subject to the control of their Inns of Court and the Senate of the Inns of Court and the Bar.

INFORMALITY:
tribunals are less
formal than
courts; no formal
rule of evidence

SPEED:
tribunals operate
more quickly
than the ordinary
courts

ADVANTAGES
OF
TRIBUNALS

FLEXIBILITY:
more flexible
than courts; not
contained by
rules of
precedent; have
a wide discretion

COST:
cheaper than
ordinary courts;
costs not
normally
awarded

SPECIALISM:
operate in
specialised fields;
possess expertise
in specific fields

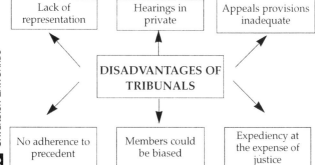

Lack of
representation

Hearings in
private

Appeals provisions
inadequate

DISADVANTAGES OF
TRIBUNALS

No adherence to
precedent

Members could
be biased

Expediency at
the expense of
justice

Other professions come under similar scrutiny by their controlling body. These tribunals possess tremendous powers. Where the tribunal has been set up by statute, an appeal will usually lie. In other cases it will depend on the willingness of the courts to get involved. The courts must apply the principles of natural justice to ensure the tribunal has not acted *ultra vires* (*Lee v Showmen's Guild of Great Britain* (1952)).

MANDAMUS: used to compel the performance of some duty, for example, to allow an appeal	*CERTIORARI:* used to compel a tribunal to inform the High Court of the facts of the case if it has acted *ultra vires*	**PROHIBITION:** used to prevent a tribunal going beyond its jurisdiction or acting wrongfully

The courts can insist that the tribunals observe the principles of 'natural justice'. Two special rules must be observed:

MANDAMUS: here, there is a duty to hear both sides before a decision is made: *Ridge v Baldwin* (1963)	*NEMO JUDEX IN CAUSA SUA:* decision must be reached after impartial and independent consideration of the evidence: *Dimes v Grand Junction Canal* (1852); *Altrincham Justices ex p Pennington* (1975)

Control of tribunals

By the courts
Courts can exercise some control over tribunals. There is normally a provision for a right to appeal on a point of law to the ordinary courts. The courts can further exercise controls over tribunals by the use of 'prerogative' orders, to ensure tribunals apply the rules of natural justice.

Control by the Council on Tribunals
This is a permanent body of up to 15 members appointed by the Lord Chancellor to review the constitution and working of administrative tribunals, and to examine rules of procedure.

The Ombudsman
An official appointed by Parliament to hear complaints from individuals who have suffered administrative mismanagement. The Ombudsman system has been introduced into banking and insurance. Under s 21 of the Courts and Legal Services Act 1990, a Legal Service Ombudsman has been appointed by the Lord Chancellor to investigate complaints about professional bodies in the legal profession, for example, licensed conveyances.

Courts with special jurisdiction
Restrictive Practices Court;

Coroners Court;

Courts Martial; and

Ecclesiastical Courts.

Future and control of the tribunal system

It is argued that control and supervision of the system cannot rest with one body alone – the Council of Tribunals. The courts do exercise some control through appeal or review, but it is stated that there needs to be a uniform code of procedure to govern the workings of tribunals which would promote more safeguards and consistency. Questions posed are:

- should the Council on Tribunals be given extended powers?;

- should its composition be altered and its resources increased?;

- should it be afforded a political base in the form of a select committee in Parliament?

Various reports have drawn attention to issues concerning the tribunal system:

- the Special Report of the Council in 1980, *The Functions of the Council on Tribunals* (Cmnd 7805); and

- the JUSTICE/All Souls Report, *Administrative Justice* (1988).

Inquiries

Inquiries are usually established on an *ad hoc* basis when it is necessary to deal with a specific issue, for example:

- to investigate major accidents by air, sea or rail;

- to investigate companies under the Companies Act; and

- inquiries into a specific event.

Arbitration

Arbitration is a means of settling disputes other than by court action and arises when one or more persons are appointed to hear the arguments put forward by the parties and to decide upon them.

Advantages of arbitration

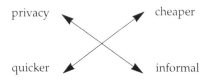

privacy — cheaper

quicker — informal

- A matter can be referred to arbitration by the court.

- A court may refer a matter to arbitration by Acts of Parliament or by agreement, if the issues concerned are complex and technical.

- Agreement can be in any form, oral or written, but the Arbitration Act only applies to agreements in writing.

- The agreement normally names the arbitrator, but the agreement can specify a specific body, for example, a trade or profession.

- The arbitrator can examine witnesses and parties concerned on oath, and require parties to submit documents, accounts, etc.

- The arbitrator makes an award, this is final – no rights of appeal, the arbitrator can order the party to pay the entire costs of the proceedings if they lose.

- Where there is an arbitration agreement and one party nevertheless brings court proceedings on the application of the other party, the court will 'stay' proceedings.

- The arbitration agreement must cover the dispute which is before the court, otherwise the court will not stay proceedings.

- The person asking for the stay must have taken no part in the court proceedings.

Procedure in arbitration

Duty of arbitrator

The duty of the arbitrator is to resolve the dispute by making an award. The arbitrator can employ a legal adviser if necessary, to help him draw up the award if he feels he is not competent to deal with the legal issues involved. The arbitrator fixes the time and place for hearing the parties and will inform them of this arrangement. If the arbitrator has specialised technical knowledge, he can dispense with the need for expert witnesses. This reduces costs.

If an important point of law arises, the arbitrator can 'state a case' for the opinion of the court. When the opinion of the court is given, the arbitrator applies the law to the facts of the case and makes his award. The arbitrator can decide that it is not necessary to 'state a case'. He can, however, be compelled to do this by one of the parties.

The award is final. However, the court can set aside an award on procedural grounds if:

Arbitrator has misconducted himself, or award obtained by improper means	Arbitrator refuses to hear one of the parties
Witnesses were examined in the absence of one of the parties	Arbitrator has been in communication with one of the parties about the issues involved

Enforcement

The party in whose favour the award has been made can enforce the award in the same way as he could a court judgment.

The Arbitration Act 1996 provides that the object of arbitration is the fair resolution of disputes by an impartial tribunal without unnecessary delay or expense. It says that the parties should be free to agree how their disputes are resolved, subject only to such safeguards as are necessary in the public interest. Courts can only intervene as far as the Act allows them to do so. In order to be governed by the Act, arbitration agreements must be made in writing. Under the Act, a party is entitled to appeal to a law court to challenge the award made in arbitral proceedings on the ground of a 'serious irregularity' affecting the tribunal, the proceedings or the award. Nonetheless, the Act greatly restricts the scope of appeals that may be made to a law court on a point of law.

7   Criticisms of the jury system

The jury is thought to be one of the most vital features of the English legal system and a fundamental safeguard to our liberty. However, the jury has been criticised over the years.

The most influential of the recent studies is Penny Darbyshire's 'The lamp that shows that freedom lives – is it worth a candle?', which was produced as a result of her experience of serving on a jury. Her aim was:

> … to question the traditional qualifications used in praise and defence of the jury, suggesting that some of them are conceptually unsound … [to] argue that jury defenders inflate the jury's importance by portraying the 'right' to jury trial as central to the criminal justice system and as a guardian of due process and civil liberties.

Darbyshire criticises the traditional view of the jury and criticises those commentators who emphasise the 'mystery' of the jury. Juries, she states, are not a representative sample of the population. She points out that they are:

> An antidemocratic, irrational and haphazard legislator, whose erratic and secret decisions run counter to the rule of the law.

The Royal Commission on Criminal Justice has put forward proposals to reduce the role of the jury in criminal trials.

Although the jury is seen to be an important cornerstone of the English legal system, few in-depth studies have been made of it. Some commentators have tended to view the jury in a romantic light, which, it is argued, is detrimental to change in the justice system.

Darbyshire's arguments tend to imply that it plays such a small role in the minority of cases, its passing would not be cause for lament.

Others argue, however, that the jury system performs a very important service and it should be protected at all costs.

The use of the jury in English law dates back into history. However, today, the use of juries has declined.

- The Administration of Justice Act 1933 limited the use of juries in civil cases.

- In 1986, the Roskill Report advocated the abolition of a right to jury trial in complex fraud cases.

- Lord Denning has argued that some jurors are not adequately suited to the task required of them.

- Reforms to the Criminal Damage Act 1971 have taken certain cases away from the jury, making them summary offences.

- Part V of the Criminal Justice Act 1988 removed the right to jury trial in other offences including driving whilst disqualified.

- In its study, *The Distribution of Criminal Business between the Crown Court and Magistrates' Courts* (1975), the James Committee recommended that minor thefts and similar offences should become summary offences.

- In civil cases, the use of the jury has almost disappeared and the Coroner's Court has been modified by the Criminal Law Act 1977.

- The Northern Ireland (Emergency Provisions) Act 1991 has taken away the right to jury trial for defendants in serious criminal cases.

- It is possible for a judge to curtail the jury by asking for a special verdict: *Bourne* (1952); *Robbins* (1988).

The Royal Commission's proposals regarding the jury will add to the curtailing of its powers in the system.

Some commentators have argued for reform of the jury along the lines of continental procedures. The Royal Commission conducted a study of pre-trial procedures used in France and Germany (Leigh and Zedner, *A Report on the Administration of Criminal Justice in the Pretrial Phase in France and Germany* (1992)), although this has not gained favour.

The 1999 jury proposals

In 1999, the government announced its intention to introduce legislation to curb the right to jury trial. In essence, it wishes, in cases triable either way, to disallow a defendant from insisting upon trial by jury in circumstances where magistrates believe that they are well suited to hear the case. More than 18,500 defendants a year would lose their right to trial by jury under these plans. The plans were advanced by the government to, according to its own contentions, speed up the hearing of criminal cases. The proposed reform was widely condemned by civil rights groups, the Bar and other lawyers.

The government decided to push ahead with the change after finding that many people who opt in the early stages of their cases for trial by jury change their plea to guilty before the trial is heard. Home Office research shows that more than 70% of those who opt for jury trial plead guilty by the day their Crown Court case opens. The average cost of a jury trial is £13,500, compared with £2,500 for a hearing by magistrates.

One Home Office paper (*Jury Trials*, 1998, Home Office) suggested that defendants elect for trial by jury at the Crown Court in an attempt to put pressure on the Crown Prosecution Service to accept a plea to a less serious charge; to make it more likely that witnesses do not turn up or be vague in their recollections; or simply to put off the day of conviction and sentence.

One problem for those who support such a change is that if, for serious crimes, you support the rigmarole of jury trials because so much is at stake for the defendant, how then can you justify removal of the defendant's right to a jury trail in cases which manifestly threaten life ruining results for a defendant? Offences like indecent assault and theft are cases in point.

The role of the jury

TO DECIDE THE FACTS OF THE CASE

They are lay persons, they have no knowledge of law and are not competent to put forward any opinion on law. They rely on their common sense to assess the accused and the evidence against him in order to reach a verdict. If the verdict is an acquittal, it is unchallengeable (there is no appeal against an acquittal)

FUNCTION OF THE JUDGE

Inter alia, to explain the law to the jury so it can reach a verdict. At the conclusion of the evidence, to sum up the case before the jury retires to reach a verdict. The judge has no judicial power to instruct a jury to convict an accused: *DPP v Stonehouse* (1978)

- Once the accused is acquitted, he cannot be charged with the same offence again. This has been criticised and was particularly highlighted during a recent case where the accused was found not guilty of murder on the grounds of self-defence (*Elliot* (1993)).

  However, Baldwin and McConville in *Jury Trials* (1979) established no evidence to suggest that juries acquitted people in the face of unjust prosecution.

- Section 36 of the Criminal Justice Act 1972 does provide for a procedure whereby points of law which arise in a criminal case where the defendant has been acquitted, can be referred to the Court of Appeal by the Attorney General to see if any loopholes in the law can be amended. This does not, however, affect the original verdict.

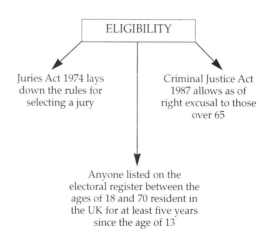

ELIGIBILITY

Juries Act 1974 lays down the rules for selecting a jury

Criminal Justice Act 1987 allows as of right excusal to those over 65

Anyone listed on the electoral register between the ages of 18 and 70 resident in the UK for at least five years since the age of 13

Members of the
judiciary

Barristers, solicitors

INELIGIBLE

The clergy

The mentally ill

The Criminal Justice and Public Order Act 1994 has disqualified people on bail from sitting on a jury.

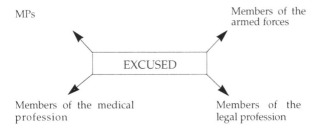

MPs

Members of the
armed forces

EXCUSED

Members of the medical
profession

Members of the
legal profession

Selection of the jury

Those entitled to be excused by administrative discretion:

- any person who has served on a jury in the last two years;

- persons with good reason to be excused (s 120 of the Criminal Justice Act 1988).

Challenging jury membership

Jury membership may be challenged if:

- the juror is in fact not qualified; or

- the juror is biased; or

- the juror may be reasonably suspected of bias against the defendant (s 12(4)).

Juries Act 1974

The prosecution has a right to challenge as well as the defence, and also has the right to ask a juror to 'stand by' for the Crown.

The Attorney General has laid down guidelines as to when the prosecution can exercise the right:

- if a jury check shows information to support exercising the right to stand by; or

- if the person to be sworn in as a juror is unsuitable and the defence agree (*Practice Note* (1988)).

Either side can challenge the array.

Peremptory challenge

In the past, the defence had the right of peremptory challenge, whereby it could challenge up to three jurors without giving any reasons. The right to peremptory challenge was abolished by the Criminal Justice Act 1988 (s 118).

Jury vetting

The panel is selected at random, and any party to the proceedings can inspect the panel from which the jurors will be chosen.

Jury vetting is the investigation of jurors' backgrounds to determine whether they are suitable for jury service.

The practice first came to public notice in 1978 during the 'ABC trial', a case brought under the Official Secrets Act 1911.

ENGLISH LEGAL SYSTEM

Two cases in 1980 highlighted the practice of jury 'settling': *Crown Court at Sheffield ex p Brownlow* (1980); *Mason* (1980).

Challenging jury membership

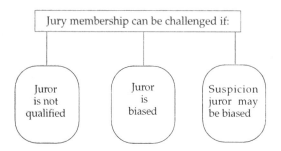

Jury membership can be challenged if:

| Juror is not qualified | Juror is biased | Suspicion juror may be biased |

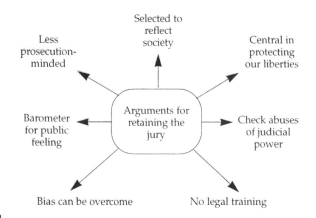

Arguments for retaining the jury

- Selected to reflect society
- Less prosecution-minded
- Central in protecting our liberties
- Barometer for public feeling
- Check abuses of judicial power
- Bias can be overcome
- No legal training

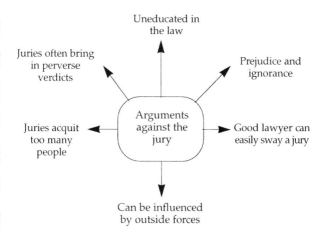

The constitutional position of this practice is much in doubt and has been criticised. However, the legitimacy and that of the Crown's right to 'stand by' potential jurors is clearly stated by the Court of Appeal in *Bettaney* (1985). The Attorney General issued a Practice Note in 1988 and also issued a statement confirming the previous guidelines.

The Runciman Commission

The Royal Commission on Criminal Justice made recommendations in order to improve the jury system:

- Section 8 of the Contempt of Court Act 1981 should be repealed to allow research into the jury.

- The Commission also made recommendations regarding the selection and disqualification of jurors.

- The Commission recommended more checks should be made of jurors to ensure they are not related to one another, or related to the accused.

- There should be more of a balance in the panel with at least three members from ethnic minority groups.

- One of these members should reflect the ethnic origins of the accused.

- Juries should be protected from outside influences during the proceedings.

- Scheduling of the trial should be more flexible to allow jurors to attend at their workplace particularly in protracted cases.

- The abolition of the defendant's right to elect for jury trial in 'either way cases'. This right should be taken from the accused and vested in the jurisdiction of the magistrates.

It is argued this would promote 'a more rational distribution of cases'.

Commentators such as McConville are deeply critical of these proposals (see 'A comedy of errors' (1993) *Legal Action*). McConville argues that, if a defendant is charged with a serious offence which could have serious implications for him, he should have the right to a jury trial.

8 Access to justice

The Access to Justice Act 1999 introduces a new structure to help people who cannot otherwise afford to use lawyers to do so. It introduces the Legal Services Commission (LSC) to replace the Legal Aid Board, and the Community Legal Service (CLS) to organise the provision of free legal services locally. The Act also introduces the Criminal Defence Service (CDS) to provide lawyers to people without sufficient means who need defence lawyers in criminal cases. These changes will not all take immediate effect in 1999/2000, so it is necessary to know something of how the legal aid system will operate during the transitional period.

The White Paper *Modernising Justice: The Government's Plans for Reforming Legal Services and the Courts* was published at the end of 1998. It proposed the most fundamental changes in the English legal system for over 40 years.

The Paper stated:

> A fair and efficient justice system is a vital part of a free society. The criminal justice system exists to help protect us from crime, and to ensure that criminals are punished. The civil justice system is there to help people resolve their disputes fairly and peacefully. This government has a radical programme of reform for the whole country. The justice system cannot be left out. We want a clearer, fairer, better system, that will make justice available to all the people.

The Paper asserted that many people are put off getting help with legal problems, because the legal system is slow, expensive and difficult to understand. It proposed a new

ENGLISH LEGAL SYSTEM

Community Legal Service that will ensure that 'people's needs are properly assessed, and that public money is targeted on the cases that need help most'.

Providing value for money in law is identified as a key aim of reform. The paper argued that taxpayers have, year on year, been paying heavily legal aid, while fewer people have been helped. By introducing contracting for legal services (the franchise system) and abolishing restrictive practices, the government aims to increase competition among lawyers and help keep costs down. It committed itself to create new avenues to justice by extending conditional fees, and modernising court procedures.

The Community Legal Service

Until recently, about £800 million a year was spent on lawyers' fees under the civil legal aid system. Another £150 million a year from local government, central government, charities and businesses is spent on the voluntary advice sector, including Citizens' Advice Bureaux, law centres and other advice centres. The government intends to set up a Legal Services Commission (to replace the Legal Aid Board) to take the lead in establishing a Community Legal Service to co-ordinate the provision of legal services in every region. The plan is to achieve control over the legal aid budget and to gradually change over to a system in which the governmental spending on legal aid and voluntary sector advice is managed from one fund.

The Legal Services Commission will manage the Community Legal Service fund, which will replace legal aid in civil and family cases.

The reasons for change

The government argues as follows. Taxpayers spend £800 million a year through the civil legal aid system on buying legal services from lawyers for those who cannot afford to pay for themselves, and this system now needs radical change.

- It is too heavily biased towards expensive court based solutions to people's problems.

- Despite a merits test, legal aid is sometimes used to fund cases that appear to be undeserving.

- It is not possible to control spending effectively. From 1992–93 to 1997–98, spending on civil and family legal aid grew by 35% from £586 million to £793 million; but, at the same time, the number of cases funded actually fell by 31% from 419,861 to 319,432.

- In the ordinary legal aid system, lawyers were paid according to the amount of work claimed for, so there is no incentive to handle cases quickly or work efficiently.

How the system will work

The Legal Services Commission will buy services for the public under contracts. Only lawyers and other providers with contracts will be able to work under the new scheme. This will enable budgets to be strictly controlled, will help to ensure quality of service, and will provide a basis for competition between different providers. The fund will be targeted on those people who are most in need of help, and on high priority cases. There will be no absolute entitlement to help, and the fund will not be spent on cases which could be financed by other means, such as conditional fees. The government does, however, intend to increase the number of people potentially eligible for advice and assistance under the scheme, to bring this into line with eligibility for representation. At the same time, those who can afford to contribute towards their legal expenses will be required to do so.

What about those who do not qualify for help from the Community Legal Service fund?

It is clear that not everyone will benefit the new scheme. In this context, the government states that it will work with the insurance industry to widen cover (it says that 17 million people are already covered by one sort of legal insurance or another, although this figure includes people entitled to legal services in respect of only one type of situation like a traffic accident or holiday disasters). It is also intended to widen the scope of the conditional fee system.

Criminal Defence Service

The government states that it will maintain the fundamental principle that those facing a criminal trial should not be afraid that lack of resources and proper representation might lead to their wrongful conviction. However, serious weaknesses in the current criminal legal aid system are identified:

The cost has rose from £507 million in 1992–93 to £733 million in 1997–98 (an increase of 44%). At the same time, the number of cases dealt with increased by only 10%. Although standard fees are now paid in many cases, the most expensive cases are paid in the traditional way by calculating the act after the event. The White Paper stated that the system gave lawyers an incentive to boost their fees by dragging cases out, and that such cases took up a disproportionate amount of money. The system for means testing defendants to see whether they should contribute to the costs of their case was seen as a waste of time and money. The test has not stopped some apparently wealthy defendants from receiving free legal aid, and 94% of defendants in the Crown Court pay no contribution.

To begin with, the CDS will be run by the Legal Services Commission, but it will be an entirely separate scheme from the Community Legal Service, with a separate budget. The Commission will develop contracts for different types of criminal defence services and implement them following pilot schemes. All contracts for Criminal Defence Services will include quality requirements, and, wherever possible, prices for the contracts will be fixed in advance. Fixed prices create an incentive to avoid delay, and reward efficient practice. Eventually, contracts with solicitors firms will cover the full range of defence services, from advice at the police station to representation in court. If a case requires the services of a specialist advocate in the Crown Court, this is likely to be covered by a separate contract. Opponents of this move argue that fixed-price work is not conducive to justice as such a system of payment encourages corner-cutting and work of an inferior standard.

Very complex and expensive cases – where the trial is expected to last 25 days or more – will not be covered by ordinary contracts. A defendant's choice of solicitor will be limited to firms on a specialist panel, and a separate contract will be agreed in each case.

Pressing questions here are whether the government will introduce a salaried defender service, and, if so, whether client choice will be limited? The government has stated that it believes that the CDS should be free in principle to employ lawyers directly to offer services to the public, as well as contracting with lawyers in private practice. The CDS will be expected to take account of the current pilot scheme involving public defence solicitors in Scotland. The government has also said that, 'in most cases', suspects and defendants will be able to choose any lawyer who has a current contract with the CDS. The fact that lawyers have a contract will also be a guarantee that they have met the relevant quality standards. In very expensive cases, where special skills and experience are often needed, the defendant's choice will be limited to those lawyers who are on a special CDS panel and have demonstrated their ability to handle cases of this type.

Lawyers however have expressed fear at this proposal. The Law Society has said that famous campaigning lawyers such as Gareth Peirce (who helped release the Guildford Four and the Birmingham Six) and Jim Nicol (who represented the appellants in the Carl Bridgewater case) might be shunned by the CDS.

Who will decide whether to grant criminal representation, and how? As now, it will be for the court to decide whether to grant a defendant representation at public expense, according to the interests of justice. But, the current requirement for a means test will be abolished. Instead, after a case is over, a judge in the Crown Court will have the power to order a convicted defendant to pay some or all of the costs of his defence. This will mean that assets frozen during criminal proceedings, and any assets which only come to light during proceedings, will be taken into account, so some wealthy criminals will pay much more than they do now.

The Access to Justice Act 1999

Under the new system, legal aid will no longer be available for:

- those seeking accident compensation (except clinical negligence cases);

- disputes about inheritance under a will or an intestacy;

- matters affecting the administration of a trust or the position of a trustee;

- matters relating to the position of directors of companies, restoring a company to the Register or dealing with the position of minority shareholders;

- matters affecting partnerships;

- matters before the Lands Tribunal;

- cases between landowners over a disputed boundary of adjacent property; and

- cases pursued in the course of a business.

The hope is that the extension of conditional fees in these areas will provide increased public access to lawyers.

The government has said it is committed to:

(1) allowing conditional fee agreements (no-win, no-fee agreements) to be used in all except family and criminal cases;

(2) transferring to conditional fees most money and damages claims currently supported by legal aid;

(3) removing most personal injury actions from the scope of legal aid;

(4) ensuring that clinical negligence cases to be conducted only by practitioners who are experienced in this field of litigation;

(5) the setting up of a limited transitional fund which would provide support in cases where there are high investigative costs in establishing the merits of a case or where the costs of carrying the case are very high.

Since 1995, 45,000 people have taken advantage of conditional fee arrangements (CFAs) to bring personal injury claims. The government has noted that many of these people would have been unable to afford to pursue their claims at all without conditional fees – people only just above the legal aid limit, people who are far from well off. These people, the Lord Chancellor has argued, are the great majority of the population who are in work – with families, mortgages, savings, or other assets – which mean that they are not eligible for legal aid, but who cannot contemplate the open ended commitment of meeting lawyers' fees.

In 1999, Lord Irvine, the Lord Chancellor, stated that the government had been listening carefully to the comments received in relation to clinical negligence cases, and accepted that many lawyers practising in this area needed time to modernise the way they run their firms so that they can take cases on regardless of their financial standing. That is why legal aid (or whatever it comes to be called under the new CLS provision) is to be retained for the time being. There is currently not a good record of claims in this area. The net cost of clinical negligence cases to the taxpayer last year was £27 million. Looking at the cases closed by the Legal Aid Board in 1996/97, 32 cases recovered £500,000 or more. Leaving these cases aside, the average cost of cases was

£4,122 to recover average damages of £4,107. In only 17% of cases was £50 or more recovered (and 1996/97 was a good year: closed case data from previous years shows recovery rates between 13% and 17%).

Clinical negligence cases are a specialist area of litigation. It can be difficult to identify at the outset whether a case has merit, and even as the medical evidence unfolds whether the negligence alleged has caused the ailment or injury. The government believes that part of the reasons for the high failure rate is that cases are being pursued by lawyers who are insufficiently experienced in this area of litigation.

The Lord Chancellor stated that the government does not propose to remove these cases from the scope of legal aid for the present. The government does intend, however, to do what it can to reduce the high failure rate of these cases. It cannot be right, it has argued, that it is only in as few as 17% of all the cases that are supported by a legal aid certificate that more than £50 is recovered in damages. Clinical negligence cases should be conducted by practitioners who are experienced in this field of litigation.

The government will establish a Transitional Fund as help will be needed during a transitional period to assist in the change of funding away from legal aid. There may be some extraordinary cases, among those categories to be removed, which lawyers may not, initially, be able to fully support on conditional fees. This fund would provide support in cases, for example, where presently, few lawyers' firms are structured financially to carry a very high costs case, because they could not afford the risks of losing, or where there are high investigative costs of establishing the merits of the case.

The fund would also provide help in those cases which we exclude from legal aid which demonstrate a significant wider public interest. This would allow the provision of assistance in this kind of case under the transitional arrangements ahead of primary legislation to establish a public interest fund. The aim of such a fund would be to support cases where there was seen to be a significant wider public interest in law on any matter and where the case would not otherwise be brought.

The consultation paper *Access to Justice with Conditional Fees* (1998, LCD) notes that it will be necessary to decide what should constitute public interest. For example, a test case about a novel point of law might have no more than a 50% chance of success, but the decision could impact on numerous future cases (in the way that recent cases involving sporting injuries have extended the duty of care owed by officials wider than was previously accepted). Or a claim for a relatively small sum in damages might benefit a large number of other people with a similar claim.

The Conditional Fees Order 1998
The right to use 'no-win, no-fee' agreements to pursue civil law claims was extended by the Conditional Fees Order 1998. The Order allows lawyers to offer conditional fee agreements to their clients in all civil cases excluding family cases. The government has argued that these agreements will result in a huge expansion of access to justice.

Conditional fees have been the means by which at least 45,000 personal injury cases have been brought, and many, in all likelihood, would not have been brought but for the existence of conditional fees. Until now, the scheme has been limited to personal injury cases; insolvency cases; and cases before the European Court of Human Rights. The new Order retains the old rule that the maximum uplift on the fees lawyers can charge is 100%, that is, a lawyer may take on an action against an allegedly negligent employer whose carelessness has resulted in the client being injured. The lawyer, who might normally charge £2,000 for such a case, can say 'I shall do this work for nothing if we lose, but £3,000 if we win'. In fact, as the price uplift can be up to 100% of the normal fee, he or she can stipulate for up to £4,000 in this example. The Law Society has recommended an additional voluntary cap of 25% of damages, and this has been widely accepted in practice over the last two years.

The main problem here continues to be that the new system, designed really to help the millions who have been regulated out of the legal aid system, does not help people whose cases stand only a limited chance of success – as lawyers will not take their cases.

Legal aid and advice

Legal aid was not available until after the Second World War; prior to that, individuals needing legal advice had to depend on the generosity of lawyers taking their case for a bare fee.

In 1903, the Poor Prisoners' Defence Act provided, for the first time, that lawyers were to be paid from public funds.

The State system of legal aid was created through a series of statutes:

- Legal Aid Acts 1949 and 1964;

- Criminal Justice Act 1967;

- Legal Advice and Assistance Act 1972;

- Legal Aid Act 1974;

- Legal Aid Act 1979 (as amended 1985);

- Legal Aid Act 1988.

Reasons for increases in legal aid

The number of recorded crimes has risen from around 1% in the 1950s to 4% in 1989. With this increased crime rate and police involvement in the criminal courts, the increase in legal costs has been inevitable.

Eligibility for legal aid

Eligibility for legal aid is dependent on the individual's financial circumstances.

Legal aid limits were set at the same level as supplementary benefits in 1974 and increased each year as a result. The Murphy Report concluded that, since 1979, more than 10 million people have lost their eligibility for civil legal aid on the basis of income.

Eligibility levels

The new levels in force in 1993 appear to reinforce that levels have been generally reduced for legal assistance. To qualify for legal advice and assistance under the Green Form Scheme, applicants are ineligible if their income or capital is above the limits, after deducting appropriate allowances.

An applicant automatically qualifies for legal aid if he is in receipt of income support, family credit or incapacity benefit. When calculating whether a person is entitled to receive legal aid, consideration is made of their savings and items of value (such as jewellery). If the applicant's disposable income is over £7,940 (£8,751 for personal injuries claims), he will not be entitled to legal aid.

The statutory charge

This was introduced to restrict access to legal aid. The statutory charge allows the legal aid fund to charge any property which was 'recorded or preserved' by the litigant during the proceedings (s 16(6) of the Legal Aid Act 1988).

The Legal Aid Act 1988

The present legislation is contained in the Legal Aid Act 1988. It enables the Lord Chancellor to make regulations which will meet the public need of legal aid. The Act came into force in 1989 and repealed all earlier legislation.

The Legal Aid Board

The legal aid scheme is administered by the Legal Aid Board which was established by s 3 of the Legal Aid Act 1988. The Board's chairman is a layperson and members of the board are chosen for their knowledge of the legal system and fiscal issues.

The Board's powers are contained in s 4 of the Act. The Board advises the Lord Chancellor on policy issues regarding legal services. The Board produces Consultation Papers.

Section 5 sets out the duties of the Board, which include reporting annually to the Lord Chancellor.

The legal aid scheme

The legal aid scheme has three main threads:

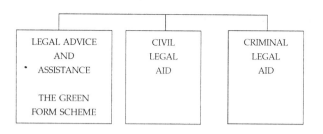

| LEGAL ADVICE AND ASSISTANCE — THE GREEN FORM SCHEME | CIVIL LEGAL AID | CRIMINAL LEGAL AID |

The Green Form Scheme

This was introduced by the Legal Advice and Assistance Act 1972 and is now contained in Pt III of the Legal Aid Act 1988. The scheme covers practical assistance from the solicitor who will advise, write letters or negotiate for the client and can consult a barrister. It covers all legal services up to (but not including) representation in court. Representation in court is further provided for in court if the client meets the necessary qualifying criteria.

Civil legal aid

Legal aid is available for proceedings in all civil courts and at some tribunals. Legal aid is available to assist with the cost of all pre-court work, including representation in court (Pt V of the Legal Aid Act 1988).

Section 15(2) of the Legal Aid Act deals with eligibility. The party must satisfy the required financial eligibility criteria. Under s 15(3) of the Act, the party must satisfy the Board that they have reasonable grounds for bringing the action for legal aid to be granted. The second limb of the qualifying criteria is linked with the 'paying client' test. That is, would a party who is able to meet the cost of the litigation after balancing the cost of the proceedings with the matter to be determined go ahead.

Criminal legal aid

Part V of the Legal Aid Act 1988 governs criminal proceedings in the magistrates' court, the Crown Court, the Court of Appeal and the House of Lords. The courts have the power to grant legal aid in criminal cases where this will be in the interests of justice.

In criminal cases, an application is made for legal aid to the magistrates; this will be decided by the magistrates' clerk. The legal aid consists of representation by a solicitor and preparation of the client's case.

Until 1982, in the Crown Courts, almost every defendant was asked to contribute to the costs and his financial circumstances were taken into consideration; any person in receipt of income support automatically qualified for legal aid.

The Legal Aid Act 1982 introduced the duty solicitor scheme in magistrates' courts. The 24 hour duty solicitor's scheme was seen as safeguarding the individual against the increase in police powers by the Police and Criminal Evidence Act 1984.

Section 22(2) of the Legal Aid Act sets out the criteria which must be met in order to decide whether to grant legal aid. Section 22 of the Act states that legal aid should be granted if the offence is likely to result in 'a sentence which would deprive the accused of his livelihood or serious damage to his reputation'.

Other criteria are:

- if the accused in incapable of comprehending the proceedings because he cannot speak English; or

- has some form of mental or physical impediment; or

- the case involves a point of law.

Standard fees
In 1993, standard fees for legal aid in magistrates' courts were introduced; this was later extended to the Crown Courts. Lawyers' remuneration is based on an hourly rate, rather than a fee for the whole case.

Legal aid franchising
The Legal Aid Board's proposal in 'Franchising: the Next Steps', has caused anxiety to the profession. Firms of solicitors who obtain a franchise will be considerably better off than those who do not. In order to apply for a franchise, solicitors' firms have to comply with the Legal Aid Board's requirements that 'systems' are firmly implemented. Specific standards must be met such as:

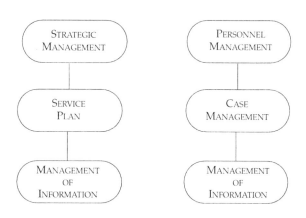

Legal aid for children

The Children Act 1989 gave children a greater say in how they are treated by the courts, particularly if the child has a sufficient age and understanding (*Gillick v West Norfolk and Wisbech AHA of the DHSS* (1986)).

Rule 9.2(A)(1) of the Family Proceedings Rules 1991 recognises the 'welfare principle' embodied in the Children Act 1989.

Children are now entitled to make their own applications to court in family proceedings. Since 1989, a child's legal aid eligibility has been based solely upon his means calculated by completing a simplified statement of means (*Re S (A Minor) (Independent Representation)* (1993)).

Unmet legal need

Vast areas of law, some with considerable importance in respect of individual rights, still remain uncovered by the legal aid scheme. Research has shown that lawyers are used only by a small social group in society, and only for a small proportion of specific area. Many individuals who would benefit from the services of a lawyer do not take advantage of the service.

The Marre Report recommended that lawyers promote more public education and awareness of the legal profession; they should attempt to be more approachable to help reduce public fear of lawyers, particularly with regard to ethnic minority groups who often feel intimidated by the legal profession.

Reform

In 1995, the Lord Chancellor spoke of the grave need to reform the legal aid system even further to stem the spiralling costs. In the Green Paper, *Targeting Need* (1995), proposals were put forward to control the amount of money available for legal services. Paying according to demand, loses favour, to a fixed annual amount for legal aid work. This type of work will be offered by those awarded a block contract under the legal aid scheme. Those that were franchised would be 'fundholders', controlling a budget and determining the allocation of funds. (This principle is already prevalent in the National Health Service.)

Alternative legal services

- Legal Advice Centres

  Normally found in Citizen's Advice Bureaux or universities; lawyers give free advice, usually regarding areas of welfare law.

- Citizen's Advice Bureaux

  The workers in the Citizen's Advice Bureau are usually trained in dealing with clients' problems, of which a great number are legally based.

Law centres

These were established in 1968 by the Society of Labour Lawyers in *Justice For All*. They were established to:

- educate the public in their rights and duties under the law; and

- specialise in specific areas of law which were seen as

appropriate to poorer sections of the community, such as landlord and tenant, employment law and social security law.

Duty solicitor's scheme

Duty solicitor's schemes are based locally, and organised by the Law Society. Volunteer solicitors attend magistrates' courts according to a rota, and interview defendants in custody who are not legally represented.